'Know, first, who you are, and then
adorn yourself accordingly.'
Epictetus

 Jordanna Levin is the bestselling author of *Make It Happen* and *Higher Love* and the host of three successful podcasts. With a background in journalism, she has built a reputation for taking 'big' topics and making them relatable, digestible and downright entertaining. Through her wit, warmth and street-smart practicality, she invites readers to get curious about the things that light them up. Jordanna believes that 'aha' moments are contagious and self-awareness is our greatest superpower. She currently spends her time writing from the sunny coastal town of Byron Bay.

Make You Happen

Manifest your best self

Jordanna Levin

affirm press

First published by Affirm Press in 2022
Boon Wurrung Country
28 Thistlethwaite Street
South Melbourne VIC 3205
affirmpress.com.au

10 9 8 7 6 5 4 3 2

 A catalogue record for this
book is available from the
National Library of Australia

ISBN: 9781922711427 (paperback)

Cover design by Alissa Dinallo © Affirm Press
Author photograph by Bayleigh Vedelago
Typeset in Minion Pro by Post Pre-Press
Proudly printed and bound in Australia by McPherson's Printing Group

Contents

Prologue

'Find out who you are and do it on purpose.'
Dolly Parton

I've got an unconventional relationship with self-help books. Truth is, I can't stand them. (If you're quickly checking the cover to make sure you picked up the right book ... stick with me, you have.) I've read a bunch of them, retained about 40 per cent of the information and put into practice about 15 per cent of that. I can recite quotes and lessons to people to sound like I know what I'm talking about but, the truth is, I've undoubtedly embodied diddly squat of those teachings to the degree I thought I would when I finished the final pages. I can recall the exact cocktail of hope, curiosity and – let's not kid ourselves – a tad of desperation as I picked up the latest self-help bestseller, thinking this could be the one that heals me, makes me feel more seen, more alive, more capable, more creative, more anything than what I currently am. A bandaid to mask whatever it is I feel like I need to fix within myself.

Full disclosure: I've actually written two bestselling self-help books. Well, that's the section of the bookstore they usually end up in, otherwise known as 'personal development' or in some cases 'spirituality', but my intention with all of my books has never been for you, the reader, to think that you need help, development or an authority on spirituality that you don't already possess deep inside of yourself. My words have always been a means for you to discover and uncover that you already have all of the answers;

I've just been so kind as to show you where to look. This is what real self-help is – guiding you back to self.

In my own life, I've been riding the personal-development train for as long as I can remember. I am a keen learner, an avid communicator and can absorb information as easily as breathing in air or gulping back that first coffee of the day. With a curious mind, a passion for finding the truth and a love for anything that makes me think outside the box, I have a tendency to chase ideas that hang out on the periphery of the masses.

I grew up around holistic therapies and spiritual ceremonies, which, at times, made them feel as everyday as a trip to Bunnings or a check-up at the dentist. They had always been part of my toolkit growing up so, as I got older, it felt like a natural progression to go deeper – to consume more and try more outlandish therapies, all in the hope of discovering some sort of magic bullet or hidden secret.

You could say there was a time when I became somewhat of a self-improvement junkie. Much like an alcoholic craves the next drink, I was never satisfied with the most recent read, alternative treatment or weekend intensive. The high that, at the time, I thought would last a lifetime, would quickly wear off within days of finishing the book, the course, the retreat, the experience and, soon enough, I would be chasing the next high, having not actually implemented any of what I just learned. I am confident that you can relate because the self-help world is a billion-dollar industry that profits off the knowledge that humans love to find faults within themselves and then seek solutions. It's the same reason the diet, fitness and fashion industries also pull in the big bucks – they profit from our own insecurities.

After decades of spiritual seeking, developing myself, searching for constant evolution and growth, and ending up working within the very industry that was profiting from my addiction, I reached breaking point. (You might know this place as rock bottom, your dark night of the soul or any of the other places we're told one must inevitably hit to have their real 'breakthrough'.) For me, it came from relinquishing any idea of being saved, fixed or healed. I ceased all of my spiritual practices, I stopped visiting my vast collection of holistic practitioners, I quit listening to self-help podcasts and reading self-help books, and I unfollowed a bunch of motivational leaders and speakers on social media.

And you know what happened? I could finally hear my own fucking voice. The little voice inside of me that had been silenced by everyone else's remedies, advice and solutions. The part of me that knows myself better than anyone else could possibly know me or ever attempt to understand me. I started to grasp an awareness of who I was without all of the hoopla. For the very first time, I met myself – in her rawness, in her nakedness – and thought, 'Wow, where have you been my whole life?' and subsequently realised that she'd been there this whole bloody time. It suddenly occurred to me that in order to maintain those highs I'd been chasing – the self-improvement, self-development, self-love and, yes, self-help – I first needed to have an acute sense of self-awareness, as without it, none of the other stuff would stick! And the sticking bit is what's important, right?

I am by no means dismissing spiritual practices, personal-development courses or even self-help books (regardless of my dramatic and fervent opener), but I've witnessed these industries – hell, I've worked for them, immersed myself in them and then subsequently stood back from them – and I can tell you that they serve you the best, and you get the most from them, when you understand that self-awareness is at the heart of all of them. Plus, when you know exactly who you are, you get to decide what concepts, theories and practices suit you and which ones just don't feel right. When I finally started to pick up some of the practices I had once dropped completely, I saw them in a new light. I found that some of them just weren't suited to me, and the ones that were very suited, well, the benefits actually stuck!

Self-awareness isn't a new topic of conversation for me. It's actually been the theme of all of my books, just in different disguises. My first book, *Make It Happen,* is about manifestation with the understanding that successful manifestation comes from having an awareness of the power of your own thoughts, feelings, action and faith. My second book, *Higher Love,* is a book about dating and relationships, pointing out that the most beneficial thing you can do for your love life is to know who you are, what lights you up and how you want to feel in love.

Now we arrive here at Book 3, and without delivering a spoiler in the first few paragraphs of said book, within these pages you will find the bones, foundations and true essence of what it means to be self-aware. Inevitably this book will end up in the self-help section, because that's the only section it fits into, but know this … you don't need to be rescued, saved or helped. You just need to get curious about who you are.

It took a lot for me to sit down and write this book. I had been teaching self-awareness for several years through the afore-mentioned guises of manifestation and love, but it was only after a series of events that resulted in a complete unravelling of the person I once was that I truly saw the significance and profound impact that an acute sense of self has on one's own ability to thrive. To explain this story in full, we need to go way back ...

I have always been a curious person, sometimes to a fault. 'But why?', 'But how?', 'Who says?' were statements hurled at my parents from as young as two years old. I recently discovered a school report card from Year 1 that said, 'Jordanna's curiosity will be her ticket to many wonderful things in her life.' My teacher was not wrong. Curiosity has led me to the most wonderful of places; deep into learnings and study, across mysterious lands searching for adventure, into thought-provoking conversations with intriguing beings and deep into internet wormholes in a bid to #FreeBritney. But of all the terrains curiosity has beckoned me to discover, none has been more transformational than my exploration into self.

In 2018 I wrote *Make It Happen*, which was born from a deep curiosity about why things happened in my life and what role I played in those happenings. In that book, I shared my fool-proof formula for successful manifestation: the Manifestation Equation. If you're unfamiliar with it or just need a refresher, it goes like this ...

Thoughts + Feelings + Actions + Faith = Manifestation

But perhaps a more accurate representation would have been:

YOUR Thoughts + YOUR Feelings + YOUR Actions
+ YOUR Faith = YOUR Manifestation

YOU are the integral piece of that manifestation puzzle and self-awareness is the backbone of your ability to manifest the life of your dreams. You see, *the only way to manifest what we want is by first acknowledging that we manifest who we are.*

In 2020 our lives came to a grinding halt with the COVID-19 pandemic (perhaps you've heard of it). Collectively, our lives began to dismantle – first in obvious ways, then in deeply personal and intricate ways as our sense of freedom was denied, our ability to progress was stalled and simple human connection was taken from us in ways we'd never consider it would be in this lifetime. Like most people, I moved through a lot of my own shit in 2020 and as people continued to read *Make It Happen,* I struggled to believe that we were capable of making anything bloody happen from the confines of our bloody houses. But in every dark moment, flickers of light begin to emerge. The true gift of 2020, when all of life's distractions were taken away, was that it gave me an opportunity to reflect on myself.

In some ways, I actually got to the end of that year knowing myself better than ever before. I had strong clarity around who I was, what I wanted out of life and what values were of importance to me. It had been a tough wake-up call, but I was incredibly grateful for everything that 2020 allowed me to see not just within myself, but in the world around me as everyone else began waking up too.

In early 2021 I suffered a great personal loss. Every little crevice of who I was, and what I stood for, vanished on me overnight. Grief dismantles you in ways you never expected. I became disconnected from who I was and my purpose, and I had no idea where to direct my energy. I struggled to articulate my needs or even communicate with people on a basic level. I lost my sense of playfulness and lightness. I couldn't even get dressed without feeling like I was pretending to be the person I was before, not the person I had morphed into seemingly overnight.

On reflection, I can now see that I was consciously detaching from myself. To be me was too painful. To get curious about what I was feeling invited emotion I wasn't ready to process. So instead, as a means of coping, I dissociated from the strong and resilient person I've always been. You could say I completely lost my sense of self, which was wildly ironic because I had just completed running an eight-week online course to a bunch of women that was all about self-awareness.

It was the recognition of this irony that puts this book in your hands today. I knew at that moment that the only one who was going to get me out of this grief and bring me back to the woman I was – even a stronger version of her – was me. Only by tapping into my own inner strengths, as well as recognising, forgiving and being gentle with my own weaknesses and taking responsibility for how my life would unfold moving forward, would I be able to get back to a life where I could make things happen!

This is not a book about grief. Nor is it a book about putting yourself back together after falling apart (although if that's why you're here, I've got you). This book is about uncovering who you are, your strengths and your weaknesses, and figuring out that you've been in possession of a bloody superpower this whole time and had no friggin idea. A superpower that, even when faced with your darkest moments, has the ability to pull you back into the light. A superpower that allows you to take ownership and responsibility for a life you're proud to live. A superpower that possesses the answers to all of your questions, allows you to make decisions with ease and communicate exactly what you mean with intention and clarity. This superpower is self-awareness and it's likely the part of your manifesting efforts that you haven't fully mastered yet, simply because you didn't know where to look.

In a way, writing this book for you so that you're able to find yourself actually allowed me to rediscover myself – and what a beautiful reunion that was. It might not sound as sexy as manifestation, meditation or masturbation (sorry, it was there so I had to take it!) but self-awareness is the heart and soul of all of those practices (yes, including masturbation – how did I end up here?). Whether you're rediscovering yourself or discovering who you are for the very first time, I am so honoured to take you on this adventure deep into YOU.

Within this book, you'll hear some entertaining tales of how I got to know myself better – yes, a lot of it was from trying some pretty crazy and outlandish practices and thera-pies – but my hope is that by recounting my stories, I am able to spark something within you. After the success of my previous books, I was acutely aware that my drawing card as a writer is bringing relatability and practicality to a book's teachings by divulging personal anecdotes and stories. Sometimes funny, sometimes embarrassing, and often requiring great amounts of vulnerability – because that's what humans connect to – but, truth be told, I couldn't even imagine what stories I'd have left to tell. Surely my 37-year bank of personal anecdotes had all been told? Turns out, I have an infinite supply of untold tales – we all do. Because the most in-depth personal-development and self-help work you can do is to experience life – make some mistakes, make a few more, endure pain, elation, heartbreak and pure bliss and, more importantly, enjoy the quieter moments and spaces in between waiting for the next big thing to drop. This is topnotch self-education. This is the crux of self-awareness. This is the Holy Grail you've been searching for your whole goddamn life. In short, self-awareness is a personal trek through your own shit (the good and the bad). This book is my trek and hopefully a comprehensive guide for you to go on your own adventure in order to make YOU happen.

CHAPTER 1

Manifesting Who You Are

*The only way to manifest what we want is by first
acknowledging that we manifest who we are.*

Ooof! Every time I read that sentence, it hits me deep in the feels. Read it a couple more times and let it sink in. It was only this year that I really understood its veracity viscerally in my bones. Writing *Make It Happen* confirmed to me what I already knew to be true – people are ready to take ownership and responsibility for making their dreams a reality. Given the right tools, people will step up to the plate and commit to creating a future they desire.

But, you see, it's the desire piece where we will often trip up. Not consciously of course, but clarity is key when it comes to manifestation and we cannot possibly know what we want and desire for ourselves unless we are crystal clear on who the hell we are AND (here is the clincher) we take full responsibility for it. It's all very well to want an abundant life, live in a big house, drive a fancy car and don a designer wardrobe, but if you're uneducated when it comes to finances, are frivolous with your savings and spend your days in a lack mentality, then what you want is bloody irrelevant. That's a really obvious and superficial example, but it's likely to strike a chord among a few of you (it certainly does with me).

Who you are, who you choose to be and who you show up as when it truly matters will far outweigh sitting down and writing your intentions for what you want to create in your life on a piece of paper under the new moon. If you are aware of yourself, embrace your strengths and weaknesses and take full responsibility for the choices you make, then, holy moly, the energy behind those intentions increases drastically! So, in this book, we're going to figure out who you are so that you can have clarity around what you want and desire in this life – because until you do, no amount of conscious manifesting will be truly fulfilling. It all comes down to self-awareness.

WHAT IS SELF-AWARENESS?

I used to coast through life with very little self-awareness. I knew who I was in terms of the things that I liked and didn't like and on some level I was conscious of how things made me feel in the moment, but I never thought to dive much further. I think this is very normal – I mean, we're not really taught what self-awareness is, let alone how to become more self-aware.

Self-awareness isn't a magic bullet or something you learn about and then instantly possess. Nor does it promise you a fuss-free, abundant or joyful life. But what it can do is create a beautiful foundation for you to understand yourself so well that you show up and embrace the world in a way that plays to all your strengths and at the same time considers your weaknesses. There is so much power in that! Self-awareness is a very personal journey, and as you read through my own adventures of self-discovery, my hope is that it sparks deep realisations within yourself about what you're truly capable of and how reflecting on your own experiences can be so incredibly eye-opening.

Much like my Manifestation Equation, which was created to demonstrate the ease and foundational principles of manifestation, I have created a three-step formula that you can apply to all aspects of your life in order to become more self-aware. But before we get there, let's just burst any quick-fix bubbles right from the get-go by saying self-awareness is a lifelong practice. Oh, I know, what a drag! In an attempt to persuade you to stick with it, though, let me repeat – self-awareness is your greatest superpower. Truly. Self-awareness is the most accessible tool you will ever have at your disposal. Having a full grasp on it will improve your life in ways nothing externally ever could. PLUS, it's free!

Before I tell you the three steps of self-awareness, as well as all of the wonderful things self-awareness is, let's have a look at all the things self-awareness is not.

Self-awareness is not:

★ Self-love or even self-care, although they're definitely by-products of being self-aware. Later in this book, you're going to learn why self-love needs to be seriously rebranded and I have a feeling that looking at it from a different perspective might just change your relationship with the elusive quest to love oneself.

★ Being aware of who you are and then ignoring good choices or purposefully stepping out of alignment with who you are. This is an act of rebellion we all experience at some point in our lives. That changes today.

★ Being aware of certain aspects of yourself and being demeaning or self-deprecating about them. But being self-deprecating is cute, right? No! Unless you're a stand-up comedian, being self-deprecating gives other people a blueprint of how you accept being treated.

★ Being defined by beliefs that limit you. Limiting beliefs … they're a bitch. Not only are they damaging to your self-awareness, they're just as detrimental to your manifestation practice. You'll meet a ton of my own limiting beliefs throughout this book and see how I overcame them. Hopefully that'll spark a little somethin' somethin' in your own belief system.

★ It's certainly not living a carefree, easy existence, where nothing goes wrong! Ha! Imagine. In this book, you'll discover that most of my profound 'aha' self-awareness moments came from my failures, but if you can gain understanding from something that seemingly failed, you can't really call it a failure at all. I think it makes it a bloody success! My hope with this book is that you learn a lot about yourself through my failures so you can do less failing and more growing.

Okay, so enough of what it isn't. What the bloody hell is it? If you're going to commit to sitting down and reading an entire book of my musings, I want you to know what promise having self-awareness holds.

Self-awareness is:

Knowing your strengths and weaknesses

… and knowing that an awareness of a weakness within yourself is actually a strength! That was a mind-blowing moment for me.

We are multifaceted beings and even the most evolved among us have weaknesses in certain areas of our lives. Instead of being beholden to a weakness or treating it as a burden, self-awareness teaches us that simply recognising and considering it gives you great strength.

Taking responsibility

This is a big one to get your head around but if you've read *Make It Happen* you're probably all over this little concept of self-responsibility. While there are some things in your life that happen to you, such as the inconvenience of a global pandemic or a natural disaster wiping out your home, there is also a bunch of stuff in your life (aka most of it) that you make happen and the only one responsible for this happenstance is you! It's a tough pill to swallow. Responsibility is your ability to respond, so when things are not seemingly working out, it's up to you to step up and decide what happens next.

Knowing when to pivot

The word pivot became quite trendy in self-help circles for a period of time there but all I think of when I hear the word pivot is Ross Geller trying to move a couch up some stairs. ('PIVOT!') *Friends* references aside (a few more might crop up, can't help it), there is a reason pivoting strikes such a chord with people – there's power in the pivot. Self-awareness allows us to spot those moments in our lives when things are no longer working and be brave enough to make the decision to go in a different direction. Which leads us to ...

Adaptability

Change is the most guaranteed constant in our lives. Change is inevitable and adapting to change can become one of the most useful tools in your tool-belt for life. Self-awareness allows you to adapt to different environments, situations and people with a lot more ease because you understand who you are, no matter what shifts in your external world.

Your unique expression

If you've ever felt like you're not being seen for who you really are or are misunderstood by those around you, it's likely that you're not expressing yourself in a way that truly reflects your authenticity. Self-awareness allows you to express yourself from a place of knowing exactly who you are and how you desire to show yourself to other people.

Having healthy boundaries

A friend told me recently that I have really healthy boundaries, which was such a compliment because I had zero boundaries for a really long time. Having no boundaries left me feeling resentful, trampled on and energetically exhausted. Self-awareness is knowing yourself so well that you're conscious of your limits and boundaries and, as an added bonus, it makes you more sensitive to other people's boundaries. Do I see healthier relationships in your future?

Practising patience

Patience is one of my biggest struggles when it comes to manifestation. Life isn't always easy and it certainly doesn't always unfold at the speed we would like it to. But self-awareness allows us to sit comfortably in the spaces between, knowing that sometimes patience truly is the wisest and most virtuous choice.

Internal validation

I could write a whole book on validation (in fact, I have carved out a section of this book to chat about it) but self-awareness teaches us that the only validation you require comes from within. This looks like giving yourself recognition rather than seeking it from others, accepting yourself rather than waiting to feel accepted by others and trusting yourself rather than putting all of your faith in others. By 'others', I mean people in your life but also all those books, programs, courses, tools and practitioners that you place all of your trust in. Looking for validation externally is a futile pursuit. A self-aware person is able to validate themselves and prioritise their own energy and emotions over pleasing other people.

Maybe you're not sure if you're self-aware or not. Here are some tell-tale signs that your self-awareness could do with some fine-tuning:

★ You repeat the same patterns over and over again.
★ You constantly seek answers and validation outside of yourself.
★ You struggle to trust your own instincts.
★ You're stuck in toxic and unhealthy relationships (romantic, platonic, business or otherwise).
★ You have never considered your own strengths and weaknesses.

* ★ You don't know how to manage your own energy and how to protect it.
* ★ You struggle with boundaries.
* ★ You lack clarity about your life path.
* ★ You don't know what you desire for your future.

If you answered yes to any of the above, then I'm so glad you picked up this book! If you answered no, then tell me your secrets, but also you're still going to gain a bunch of insights into yourself within these pages.

Here are some of the benefits you're likely to experience once you become more self-aware:

* ★ You'll be able to tune in to your own authenticity. This puts you into alignment and when you're in alignment, things fall into place, opportunities open up and you become magnetic. Woo hoo!
* ★ Your manifestation practice will improve. Which is why we're here, right?
* ★ You'll have clarity when you communicate.
* ★ You'll feel more seen and understood than ever before. Hallelujah!
* ★ You'll be conscious of your energetic limitations and, as a result, have more energy.
* ★ You'll know how and when to assert boundaries. Yes please!
* ★ Your self-worth, self-esteem and self-belief will increase. Bonus!
* ★ You'll find it easier to make decisions (because you won't have to run them past a million different people first).

* You'll be able to recognise your strengths and weaknesses.
* You'll feel more fulfillment and satisfaction.
* You'll feel less guilt and regret.
* You'll notice that the glass appears half full (rather than half empty) more often.
* Your relationships will improve.

Can I hear a 'hell yeah' to all of the above?!

THE SIX ASPECTS OF SELF

We are multifaceted beings; there are so many layers to oneself that I can find it quite overwhelming to explain self-awareness as a whole. Asking 'Who are you?' is a great place to start but that question is as loaded as they come. We are made up of a culmination of emotions, energy, thoughts, beliefs, physicalities, triggers, talents, wisdom, dreams and forms of expression, and the amalgamation of all of those factors is unique to each one of us.

So being the practical, break-it-down-as-best-I-can kinda gal that I am, I have split self-awareness into six distinct aspects. I found that when I was able to get curious, accept and embody these key areas of self, not only did I understand myself better but I also gained a clear understanding of how I showed up in the world. The six aspects are:

1. Identity
2. Emotions
3. Energy

4. Communication

5. Love, Sex & Desire

6. Spirituality & Intuition

As you progress through this book, we're going to unpack each of these aspects in detail. You'll hear a bunch of stories from my own adventures in discovering who I am through each aspect, but you'll also find exercises that will allow you to discover who YOU are. By the time you reach the end of this book, you're going to know yourself so well, but you'll also have figured out all of the answers, solutions and potential outcomes to your most pressing questions, riddles and dilemmas.

As I said before, self-awareness is a lifelong practice (yawn), and to maintain that longevity, I have found there are three really simple steps for applying self-awareness to any situation. If you follow these three steps in sequential order, they will not only lead you to a greater sense of self-awareness, but the best bit is they can also be applied to any situation or area of your life. Consider these three steps your golden path that, when followed correctly, will lead you directly back to you and the future you are responsible for creating.

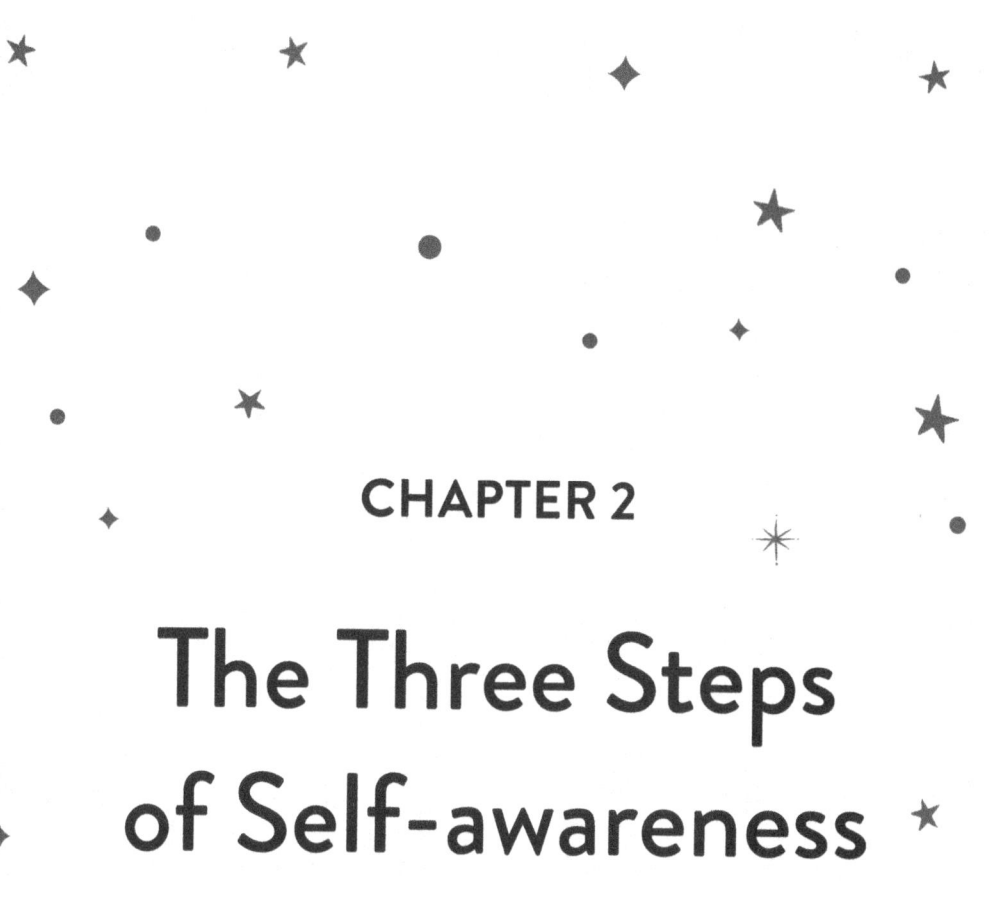

CHAPTER 2

The Three Steps of Self-awareness

The three steps of self-awareness wasn't a tool I designed so that I could become more self-aware (although that's how you're going to use them). I had actually spent three-and-a-half decades of my life taking the longest route possible towards self-discovery, without conscious knowledge of the value of this simple three-step process. My addiction to personal-development work, a bunch of missteps due to my complete lack of self-awareness and eventually a return back to self is what enabled me to look at what the most important components of discovering self were. It also made me wonder if it was possible to achieve the same level of self-awareness without having to jump through all of the self-help hoops (and truthfully tripping over a few on my way through).

This contemplation led me to two revelations: firstly, the 'hoops' are what we call experiential learning so I would never want to remove them from your orbit. In fact, my hope for you is that you allow yourself to jump through personal-development hoops to your heart's content because this is where the deepening of self-awareness takes place. However, what I experienced for several years is that I would recognise something within myself after reading a self-help book, sitting in ceremony or spending hours with my kinesiologist and then swiftly forget about it a few days later, consciously ignore it if it wasn't a favourable discovery or, alternatively, use it as an excuse for why I was who I was, as if I had no role in changing it. This is not self-awareness (well, not in its entirety anyway).

This is where the three steps come in handy because they lead you through the entire process of self-awareness – from discovery to recognition and acceptance to integration. Secondly, I realised that if there was a means by which to analyse oneself and grow from it (which the three steps allow you to do), perhaps there would be less of a desire to seek external personal-development tools in the first place because you already have everything you need at your disposal.

The three steps of self-awareness are:

1. Curiosity
2. Acceptance
3. Embodiment

Write them down, memorise them and get them tattooed somewhere you can see them (so not on your arse), because if you want access to this superpower I keep alluding to, these are the steps you need to take to get there. A complete practice of self-awareness is a culmination of all three steps combined. Consider them a blueprint to self-discovery and the more you use them, the easier the path becomes to follow. In fact, by using these three steps as a guide, I reckon by the end of this book you will have discovered so much about yourself that these steps will just become an intrinsic part of who you are.

Let's dive into each of the three steps separately so you can understand the importance of each component. Then, I'll show you how they work together as a step-by-step guide to greater self-awareness. How does that sound? Are you pumped? Fab, me too! Let's do this.

STEP 1: CURIOSITY

If curiosity really killed the cat, I would be very much a goner (that is if I am the cat in this proverb and, for argument's sake, let's say I am). We've already established that I've been led by curiosity for as long as I can remember, but the nature of being curious isn't always framed in a positive light. The aforementioned proverb warns of the dangers of unnecessary investigation and experimentation. It suggests that a curious person is sticking their nose where it doesn't belong and that asking questions outside of what is presented to you is asking for trouble, but asking questions is when real breakthroughs happen.

If we zoom out from ourselves for a minute and take a look at the shifts that have been happening on a macro level worldwide over the past few years, we've seen history-altering social movements occurring simply because people decided to start asking questions regarding things that had been silenced, swept under the rug or simply ignored for far too long. Great examples of this are the #MeToo movement, Black Lives Matter, gender equality, vaccination hesitancy and, yes, we can even attribute the rise of conspiracy theories to the fact that more and more people are questioning what and who we've always deemed as an authority. While I am by no means a conspiracy theorist (although I'm still a little suss on Princess Diana's death), I do think it's a healthy human tendency to question information that doesn't add up.

If we zoom back into our individual micro worlds, look at the things that perhaps we took as gospel and then realised over time was just a bunch of baloney once we began to question it, we can see the danger of not asking questions. Never could this be more true than when it comes to our own self-enquiry. Have you ever stopped to question your own set of beliefs? I'm not talking about whether you believe in aliens or not (but do you? Tell me, I'm undecided). I'm talking about the limiting beliefs or ideas you have about yourself that you've cultivated over time that have become the framework by which you see yourself, judge yourself and use to regulate your own potential.

Throughout this book I'm going to ask you to constantly question your own beliefs, not as a means to fill you with self-doubt but so that you can start to peel back the layers of limiting beliefs you subconsciously created that have been, well, for lack of a better word, limiting you. In *Make It Happen*, we explored the detrimental effects that limiting beliefs have on your manifestations and the future you wish to create for yourself but when it comes to self-awareness and realising your own potential, limiting beliefs completely blind you to how bloody amazing you are!

Curiosity will be the main focus of this book. As we move through the six aspects of self-awareness, I'm going to invite you to go full detective on yourself. You'll be asking yourself 'who?', 'what?', 'where?', 'why?', 'when?' and 'how?' like never before and you'll see how some simple self-enquiry opens up parts of yourself that you never even knew were available to you. You might not always have the answer, but by simply questioning it you've already opened yourself up to the fact that there is likely more to the situation you find yourself in than what you witnessed at first glance. This line of self-enquiry might come naturally to you, a regular ol' Inspector Morse, but not all of us are curiosity seekers (until now, that is). Whether you fall into the latter category or 'yeah, but why?' is your middle name, you will get ample opportunities throughout this book to get curious, and if self-awareness is your end goal (hint: it is), then it's important that you take all of the invitations I give you.

Determining your strengths and weaknesses

In *Make It Happen*, I introduced you to four universal laws. They were the Law of Attraction, the Law of Vibration, the Law of Action and the Law of Rhythms, which essentially made up what you now know as the Manifestation Equation. Well, now I'd like to introduce you to the Law of Polarity.

The Law of Polarity states that a whole is made up of two opposites that complement each other into a sense of completion. No matter how bloody wonderful you are, humans are innately made up of strengths and weaknesses; all things in the universe are. It's the fact that both your light and shade coexist that makes you a whole person. If we were to strive to eliminate all the weaker parts of ourselves, then our strengths would likely lose their weight and credibility. I believe wholeheartedly that by simply having an awareness of what your weaknesses are, you instantly transform them into strength. So that's what we're going to do throughout this book.

As we visit each aspect of self-awareness, you're going to get curious about where your strengths lie (and lean more towards them) and at the same time get curious about what your weaknesses are, not so you can use them as an excuse or a crutch but so you can be gentle with yourself, allow yourself leniency and make room for your weaknesses to exist without judgement. As someone who needs to excel at everything she does, I have found that one of my biggest teachings in this lifetime is to learn to embrace my shortcomings just as much as my strengths. The growth in that has been exponential for me and I guarantee it will be just as profound for you. When we get curious about our own strengths and weaknesses, we gain precious information about ourselves. Knowledge is power and with power comes great responsibility. The next few steps involve taking the wisdom we have gained and doing the work necessary to integrate it so that we can be the embodiment of a self-aware person. But before we move on, there is one last component of curiosity that we must explore: self-reflection.

Self-reflection

We have so much bloody distraction in our lives. Wouldn't you agree? Between Netflix, our favourite podcasts, endless social engagements and all of life's obligations, we have very little time to sit in nothingness without digital, visual, audible and social distractions. It's no wonder that simple self-reflection has become low on many of our priority lists.

Socrates once said, 'The unexamined life is not worth living.' So let me ask you, when was the last time you sat down (or stood, I'm not fussed on your positioning) and examined the happenings in your life? Simple questions like, 'How does this make me feel?', 'Why did I react that way and how would I prefer to react in the future?', 'What is this experience teaching me?' and 'What have I learned in the past that could help me navigate this situation?' are all lines of questioning that allow you to emotionally, intellectually and spiritually evaluate your life as a moment-by-moment practice. If you don't take the time to reflect on your behaviours, feelings, thoughts, motivations and desires as they arise, you can find yourself stuck in situations or headed in directions that were never part of the plan in your life.

Never has this been more important than when it comes to your manifestation practice. Manifestation in its most simple form is about taking ownership of a future you desire but in order to do that it's vital that you first get clear on what your future looks like and, secondly, that you check in with yourself consistently to make sure that you're aligning your thoughts, feelings, actions and faith with your intention. Simply pausing and asking yourself, 'Am I in alignment or out of alignment with the future I desire?' is a powerful self-reflection strategy I use daily.

Practising self-reflection takes intention, consistency and discipline. It requires you to set aside time during the chaos of your life to evaluate, ponder and feel into the role you're playing in your life and how you intend to play that role going forward. In the context of this book, we'll be using self-reflection as part of getting curious about every facet of what makes you you. Very swiftly, you will be able to gain a new perspective on old patterns and experiences, you'll be able to respond rather than just react and you'll learn more about yourself and understand yourself in ways you never have before. This is exciting, right?!

STEP 2: ACCEPTANCE

In order to be a self-aware person, you have to be able to accept every part of yourself that you discovered when you got hella curious about who you are. Until you are able to accept all of your strengths and weaknesses, you'll likely struggle to integrate and embody them and thus become fully self-aware (which, FYI, is our end goal here).

Acceptance begins with acknowledgement

After much consideration, I've discovered that a vital component of acceptance is to first acknowledge that something exists. To acknowledge is to recognise the existence and importance of something, so in the case of self-awareness, it's the existence and importance of your unique thoughts, feelings, behaviours and qualities. You can do all the digging, highlighting of your own strengths and weaknesses and analysing of your thoughts, feelings and actions as you like but unless you can acknowledge that all of these things are intrinsic parts of who you are, then all that excavating you did is redundant.

I have found in my time as an observant human that people struggle with acknowledging their strengths just as much, if not more, as their weaknesses. Have you ever dismissed a compliment, failed to celebrate a success or fallen into a stand-up comedy routine of self-deprecation? I am guilty on all three charges (especially the last one) and it's likely you are too. But you see, it's not our fault. We have existed in a world where we're told that our ego is the enemy, to accept a compliment makes you arrogant and to celebrate your own success makes you boastful. Unfortunately, because self-acknowledgement is often mistaken for being self-centred, this forces us to turn to the external to be acknowledged and validated for the things that are well within our means to acknowledge and validate ourselves (we'll explore this deeper in Chapter 8).

But that way of thinking changes now! As we move through this book, you're going to be acknowledging ALL parts of yourself. This entails embracing your strengths and weaknesses with equal enthusiasm, because if we revert back to the Law of Polarity, it's the combination of the two that makes you a whole person. The simple act of acknowledging yourself aligns you with your authenticity, increases your self-worth, inspires and encourages you, gives you valuable insights into your own motivations and gives you permission to be proud of your own achievements. Also, I believe from a spiritual perspective that when we acknowledge all of ourselves, the light and the shade, it gives the universe an opportunity to acknowledge us too.

When I first started to strengthen my self-awareness practice, I found the acknowledgement component the trickiest, so it would be unfair of me to assume that you're going to find it easy breezy. It can be difficult to acknowledge the parts of yourself that keep you stuck and equally the parts of yourself that have the potential to propel you forward but that's why I'm here. I recognise that it can be hard to navigate on your own, especially when you can't even see certain parts of yourself because they're so buried in limiting beliefs and hidden behind your own protective walls. Often when we condemn someone for not having any self-awareness, it's because we see things in them that we refuse to acknowledge within ourselves. It's a tough pill to swallow, but that's all of us to some degree (less so for those of us who follow these three steps – woo hoo, go us!) and my intention with this book is to get you to look at all sides of yourself so nothing goes unseen. Sound good, if not a little terrifying? Great, let's move on.

Be at peace with yourself

The kind of self-acceptance we will be striving for in this book is the non-discriminatory embracing of one's whole self – both strengths and weaknesses. You'll likely find it a relief to learn that I don't expect you to be accepting of every single piece of yourself. It's an unrealistic task (I am all about realistic expectations), and when we believe something to be achievable, we're more likely to accomplish it. Nor should you feel like a passive bystander. It feels extremely submissive to just learn things about yourself and think, 'Oh well, that's my lot in life. No point in trying to grow or change, I'll just accept that I am this way.' True self-acceptance isn't passive or submissive, it is about being mindful of what is true for you in the moment. Acceptance is about the removal of doubt and judgement so you can redefine your qualities as neither good nor bad, fair or unfair, successes or failures, but simply as is.

A common roadblock to self-acceptance is that many of us can only accept ourselves to the degree that we feel accepted by others. The three steps of self-awareness take you through the necessary process of self-acceptance without you needing to feel acknowledged or accepted by anything outside of yourself. As you progress through the chapters on the six aspects of self, you will find that accepting all facets of yourself will initiate great shifts in perspective of not just who you are at your most authentic but also what you're truly capable of.

When we are in resistance and refuse to accept ourselves as we are, it makes it near impossible to initiate growth or improvement, and when it comes to your manifestation practice, a resistance to self stunts manifestation completely. Repeat that again and let it sink in. You see, in order to make yourself truly magnetic, you need to be vibrating on a frequency that will attract things with a similar frequency towards you – this is the Law of Vibration. To manifest who you are and start vibrating at your own personal and authentic frequency, you need to be able to completely embody self-awareness, which brings us to the last step.

STEP 3: EMBODIMENT

Just as the Manifestation Equation requires all four parts working together in order to successfully manifest, the same goes for the three steps of self-awareness. The order of the steps holds significant weight and if you get through the first two steps but fail to truly embody the learnings gained from practising self-awareness, well, I hate to break it to you, but the whole thing falls apart.

To embody something is to be an expression of or give a tangible or visible form to an idea, quality or feeling. In the context of self-awareness, it's about being the tangible expression of what you've learned, acknowledged and accepted within yourself on a physical, emotional, energetic and spiritual level. Embodying self-awareness informs your actions and behaviours and this becomes evident in the way you express yourself, treat yourself, honour yourself and choose to show up as your most authentic self every day – and that, my friends, is the clincher. It's all very well to get curious about who you are, acknowledge your strengths and weaknesses and be at peace with them but if you want to create change in your life and manifest a future you truly desire, then you must be a living and breathing embodiment of your own self-awareness practice.

This will be a continued stretch task for you throughout this book. At the end of each of the six aspects of self, I will suggest ways for you to embody what you've learned in that chapter. Unless you take these into consideration and allow your self-awareness to be reflected in your actions and behaviours, you're just another self-help junkie who is looking for their next fix but not actually doing 'the work'. I'm being blunt and direct with you because that was me for a really long time and I don't want you to suffer the same fate. You hear me? We're all guilty of not always embodying all the wisdom we learn and spruik to others but that changes today.

Using the three steps of self-awareness in this book

The majority of this book will focus on the first step: curiosity. It's my specialty and I have all of the exercises you need to look into every nook and cranny of who you are. At the end of each chapter, we will recap what you've learned and how the three steps of self-awareness can ensure you learn the most you can about yourself in each of the six aspects.

Before we move forward to the juicy content that's going to transform your life, I want you to make a commitment to yourself here and now that you will do the exercises in this book that allow you to get curious about who you are, you will acknowledge and accept what you discover (I'll be there along the way to help you with this) and, most importantly, you will do your best to take everything you've learned and allow it to be reflected in your actions and behaviours. Deal?

It's from this place that you're able to access your authentic self. We'll explore authenticity, or as I like to call it, your personal vibration, in more depth in the next chapter, but know this: your personal vibration is the key to making you a magnet for everything that is in your highest interest because it is a direct reflection of who you are. As we move through the six aspects of self-awareness, you will begin to embody everything you discover about yourself in each aspect. By the end of this book, you will be in the best position you've ever been in to create a life you truly desire.

THE SIX ASPECTS OF SELF-AWARENESS

CHAPTER 3

Identity

Have you ever had an identity crisis? I've had several. They're usually instigated by a wardrobe meltdown, a relationship ending, a 'fat' day or a career pivot. In fact, what I have learned on the road to becoming more self-aware is that you only ever have a crisis of identity when you are identifying yourself by external means.

Whether we care to admit it or not, we are all judgemental AF! We encounter a fellow human and even before words and gestures have been exchanged, we are instantly forming a picture and opinion of who this person is. We start out basic by assuming someone's gender, which before we were all better informed about the fluidity of gender was a safe bet. We then move on to physical appearances, which can incorporate so many inaccurate assumptions. A person's race, which we cannot be so ignorant to decide based on the colour of someone's skin. We notice their body type (usually in comparison to our own), which then leads us to an assumption of their exercise routine and diet choices, with no actual proof to back up our wildly unfounded judgements. We make observations about what they're wearing, and their choice of clothing leads us to assume certain aspects of their personality, social standing or financial earning bracket. Then, perhaps, we start to learn more about them – what they do for work, where they live and who they socialise with. Their personality traits and interests begin to emerge and from here we can form what we feel, as an outsider, is a complete representation of this person. But is it? Umm no, friends, it's not. But it doesn't stop us, does it?

Let me ask you, do you think it would be accurate for someone to identify you by any of the aforementioned attributes? 'HELL NO!' I fiercely typed onto this page while sitting in a hipster cafe half dressed for a morning of exercise (that I had no intention of doing) and half dressed as a Peruvian Sherpa wrapped up in a patchwork blanket I found in the boot of the car. I was just sporting the items of clothing that were thrown into the not-dirty-enough-to-wash pile on my bedroom floor but if someone were to make assumptions on this morning's attire, I might be branded as a sporty type (which I'm not) who just got back from her travels to Machu Picchu (which I didn't) and has zero sense of style or proficient laundry liquid (which isn't entirely false).

As ridiculous as it sounds when put into context, the truth is we all do it. I've been identifying myself by my own fashion choices, work successes and the suburb that I live in for as long as I can remember – and that was consciously. Subconsciously, the list of identifiers goes much deeper. My personal journey with identity has been a long and treacherous road but taking that obstacle-ridden ninja warrior course made me realise a very simple truth: all of these things are an *expression* of our identity, not who we are intrinsically.

Being able to separate the two enabled me to cultivate my inner world to a standard I wished to be identified with. It's also imperative to be aware that your identity is not fixed; it's forever changing. With every trauma, every life-altering conversation, every success, every time the moon changes phase, fragments of who we are morph and transform. Essentially, our identity is our connection to self, and self-awareness shows us that the self is in a constant state of flux. But in order to relax into its fluidity, it's imperative that we understand just how superficial we all bloody are.

SUPERFICIALEXPIALIDOCIOUS

I like to think I'm a woman of depth. I read books, I watch documentaries, I donate to charities, I have morals and pretty high standards, I love thought-provoking conversation and philosophical contemplation and, when it comes to the procurement of 'things', I would never deem myself materialistic (she types as her fourth online order this week arrives on her front doorstep). I have full conscious awareness that appearances aren't everything, and that it's what's on the inside that counts, but I would be lying through my (recently whitened) teeth if I was to tell you that I don't judge a person by their proverbial front cover. You do it too … admit it! You are forming an impression of a person's body shape, hairstyle, fashion choices and yeah, maybe even their teeth without even being conscious of it. It's not your fault. It's decades of influential marketing and advertising that subliminally enters our impressionable sponge-like brains through our phones, TVs, billboards and peers.

For me, it started with magazines. I picked up my first one around the age of three. My mother used to own a hair salon and I would spend countless hours in there flipping through the weekly women's tabloids and the monthly glossies. It was a harmless distraction at the time, but slowly, subconsciously, I began to form a picture in my mind of how a woman should identify herself. By the age of 13 up until, well honestly to this day,

I believed, like most women, that if my body could look a certain way then people would see me differently, doors would open and everything in my life would fall into place (I've admittedly had the same thoughts about a coveted clothing item I just had to have). But the problem with this goalpost that we are all set on reaching is that it's always bloody moving.

Poor Jen

I recall sitting at a doctor's surgery watching a young girl, barely a teen, flip through a copy of *Marie Claire* magazine with Jennifer Aniston on the cover. I think anyone who was emerging as a woman in the 90s and early 00s will know the goalpost that was Jennifer Aniston's abs. Every weekly and monthly magazine featured her diet plan, exercise regimen, latest hairdo and effortless style. In retrospect, 'the Rachel' was possibly the worst hairstyle to come out of the 90s, and this was the decade that brought us the half-crimped, half-straight, half-up, half-down hairdo, so that's really saying something. (If you were one of the victims that rocked the Rachel, I pray there's no photo evidence to incriminate you.)

As a 16-year-old, I kept a magazine clipping of Jen and her beau Brad (heard of him?) on the inside of my wallet – ya know, where you're meant to pop a photo of your loved ones? Brad looked effortlessly hot in his baggy grey T-shirt and army-green cargo pants, and Jen sported her signature orange cargo pants rolled up at the ankles and a fitted black tank top. Her tiny and toned arms, her impossibly flat belly and the slight jut of her hip bones became the aspirational image that I'd use to guilt myself into forgoing a sandwich at lunchtime.

I have seen all ten seasons of *Friends*, no joke, about 15 times from start to finish. I could listen to an episode of *Friends* like a podcast and be able to visualise exactly what is happening on the screen. I distinctly remember, however, the first time Season 8 aired (in real time, not one of the 15 re-watches). All of a sudden, my enjoyment of *Friends* began to shift from a half-hour of entertainment to intense scrutiny of Jen's outfits and impossibly slim physique. I no longer saw Rachel Green, girlfriend of Ross who was definitely not on a break. I saw Jen and her daily yoga sessions, running regimen and effortless willpower to avoid carbs at all costs. Do you think Jen knows the impact she had on women's insecurities the world over? Surely she does, although none of it was her fault. She was simply existing in an industry that used her genetics to pedal their own consumerist agenda. It's actually so fucking wild to think about.

'Poor Jen', the tabloids screamed when Brad left her for Angie or when her marriage to Justin ended after just two years. 'She never had children and never managed to keep a man, but boy did she manage to keep those abs.' Twenty years later, and Jen's influence hasn't diminished. The women who worshipped her in their 20s are still worshipping her in their 40s. Is that a burden that Jen has had to bear? If she can't impress people with her fairytale ending, then at least her body still looks like it did when she was 25? The pressure!

Can you imagine the weight of knowing that you were the aspirational image plastered inside girls' lockers, on the cover of exercise books and pinned to women's fridges to deter midnight snacking? She never asked for this, poor Jen. She didn't know when she chose to be an actor that she would influence what women would eat, how they would move and what they would choose to deprive themselves of in order to look just like her. As I looked over at this barely teen who, let's be honest, was not interested in 50-year-old Jen, I wondered who her impossible goalpost was. What food group would she deprive herself of in order to look just like her and, equally, what lengths had that celebrity goalpost gone to in order to become the poster girl for body perfection in 2021?

In the 90s, when I was obsessed with teenage glossies, I thought I had discovered a secret manual to being a woman. We all bloody did! How to dress, how to flirt, how to understand your body better, how to exercise, how to diet, how to practise self-care. To the oblivious consumer, these magazines did offer so much. But at the same time, they were also doing the direct opposite. They were taking away our power to discern what beauty was, what healthy looked like and the benefits of exercise that existed outside of weight loss. What I thought was a monthly indulgence – a quiet afternoon of self-care as I lay in the sun and flipped through its pages – was slowly destroying any kind of sovereignty I would have around who I was and how I compared to this magazine's portrayal of perfection.

This isn't a new conversation. In fact, it's a conversation I'm bloody bored of having. As adults, we're fully aware of the poor body image we've inherited through the manipulation of our insecurities from the diet industry, the under-representation of body diversity and the silence of celebrities and models when it comes to the extremes they must go to in order to achieve perfection.

But has our awareness of it made a difference to our consumption and reaction to it? Does having an awareness that you can't realistically achieve a bikini body in five days make us any less inclined to try? It is, of course, a very different landscape now. The question of magazines and their detriment to our mental health is really no longer the issue (excuse the mag pun). The world in which this sweet girl holds 52-year-old Jennifer Aniston in her hands is a very different world to the 32-year-old Jennifer Aniston I held in my hands. Her Jen equivalent isn't just found in magazines, it infiltrates all of her devices. As much animosity as I have for the insecurities magazines awarded me, I grow nostalgic for static images, 'unknown' sources and the ability to shut the magazine and walk away.

These days, things are different. The Jens of today let you into their homes via selfies and homemade movies, their lunch is documented in real time and if you want to know their workout routine, well why not join in via live stream? There is no hearsay, there is direct face-to-camera action and it hunts you down waiting to pounce on you when you're at your most vulnerable. The advertisers that took up double-page spreads in your favourite magazine now follow your every move in unsuspecting places. Social media posts are targeted to your specific insecurities. Your weaknesses are amplified and hand delivered through quantified remedies. There is no hiding and no sovereignty when it comes to deciding who you are or who you desire to be. No, they have already decided that for you.

As I sat in that waiting room staring down this young teen, I knew she was already fundamentally influenced by the industry that my fellow peers and the generations before us had supported. I saw my younger self in her shoes – the young girl who treated those magazines like gospel because she didn't know any better.

I pondered what would have made a difference to me back when Jen's abs were my Holy Grail. Would it have been Jen declaring her genetics played a big part and that she was miserable without the indulgence of a fresh croissant on a Sunday morning? Yeah, I bloody reckon it would have! Had I known that no matter how hard I worked and how little I ate I would never achieve that physique, I may have focused my efforts on nurturing my body rather than berating it. Would a greater representation of women's bodies in the magazines that held Jen to an impossibly high standard have helped me embrace my own body? Mmm hell yeah!

Yet I look at the body positivity and body diversity that's slowly integrating its way into fashion brands, onto catwalks and infiltrating social media, and still I question if it makes the industry more inclusive or if it's a tokenistic gesture that further highlights the disparity we've experienced for decades and is now permanently ingrained in our psyche. We have to be doing better and, unfortunately, it can't be left to the industries who profit from our vulnerabilities. It starts with you and me reminding our kids, reminding our friends, reminding teens in doctors' waiting rooms devouring airbrushed images of Jen and reminding ourselves that this is not real life nor should we want it to be.

Can I let you in on a little secret? I spent two weeks trying to make this section of the book sound light and funny. I thought Jen Aniston and *Friends* references might do the trick, but the harsh reality of what you just read is that our connection between body image and identity is no laughing matter. I'm serious! Me, the self-deprecating gal who prides herself on making any topic a stand-up comedy routine, wants to emphasise the preposterous nature of the media's influence on the unachievable standards by which we choose to identify. I mean, I guess it's funny in a ludicrous way, but in a haha way? No siree.

My respite in times of complete body-image overwhelm comes in the form of Celeste Barber. For those of you not familiar with her work, she is an Aussie comedian and media personality who rose to fame on Instagram in 2015 with the hashtag #celestechallengeaccepted. Now sporting more than 8 million followers, Barber has built a reputation for creating parodies of celebrities and models. It shines a very realistic lens on the over-fabricated and digitally manipulated world that we live in. Even though I don't wish to take any of this too seriously, and I do profess that we call her Queen Celeste, it's so disappointing that it takes a woman to make herself the butt of the joke and constantly point out her own 'flaws' for us to understand that the real flaws are in our perception of our bodies, not in our bodies themselves.

We've arrived at our first exercise in self-reflection. You'll need your self-awareness journal for this exercise. All I ask is that you are brutally honest with yourself in the following exercises. Writing down what you think is the right answer, rather than how you really feel, will benefit nobody (but especially not you).

Exercise 1
LET'S GET CURIOUS ABOUT OUR BODIES

It's time to get curious about what role your physical body plays in how you present to the world and equally how the world sees you.

Gentle reminder: your body image 'stuff' is likely not your fault. It's decades of being told how you're meant to feel about your body.

Equally gentle reminder: there's absolutely nothing wrong with using your body to express who you are, as long as it's aligned with who you are on the inside (which is what we'll explore throughout this chapter).

Answer the following questions:

1. If I had to describe how I feel about my body in one sentence, how would I describe it?

2. What do I perceive to be the ideal body and how does my body differ from this ideal?

3. Where did I develop the belief that there was a 'perfect' body to strive for? For example, magazines, social media, social circles, etc.

4. Are there parts of my body that I use to create my identity? For example, I've always thought my hair was an important aspect of who I was. I discovered that I placed way too much importance on my hair as a way of presenting myself to the world. Again, this is not wrong, just something to be aware of within yourself.

5. What assumptions about me do I believe people make based on my physical body? Note: I'm asking what *you* believe, not necessarily what's true.

6. If I took away all aspects of my physical body as a means of identity, what would I be left with? (There's no right or wrong answer here, but it'll set us up moving forward.)

So, hopefully by unpacking just how much of an emphasis we place on the physical as a means of identification, you are able to open up to the idea that perhaps there are more valuable ways to identify as you. Before moving inward, there are still a few superficial expressions of our identity that we need to address first. But before we do, I feel like I must clear up my definition of superficial in this context. I am by no means using the word superficial to describe you or I as someone who lacks depth of character or understanding. That would be RUDE and simply untrue. In this context, I am referring to the external means by which we identify – so superficial as in the surface level, not shallow or artificial. We clear?

Farshun!

I'd never deem myself to be particularly fashion forward, but from a very young age I've been conscious of the fact that the clothes I choose to wear are a direct reflection of how others will perceive me. There are photos of me in 1988 at the tender age of four sporting a geometric printed shorts and T-shirt ensemble, and I look bloody miserable. I clearly remember the day these photos were taken. 'Girls don't wear shorts!' I tried to explain to my dad who had gifted me this (on reflection) *très* cute outfit.

You have to remember this was the 80s. I wasn't well versed in the concept of gender fluidity like the four-year-olds of today and I certainly didn't have the foresight to know that my 37-year-old self would kill to be able to pull off a similar pair of short shorts. But what I was certain of was that by wearing those shorts, people would identify me as something I wasn't willing to portray – a boy, because I wasn't. I was a girl and, in my mind, my clothing choice was a heavy enough influence to persuade them otherwise. In hindsight that seems ridiculous, but is it?

Throughout my entire life, I've been conscious that the clothes I slip into that morning will not only influence and/or alter people's perceptions of me, but also that they are an expression of who I choose to show up as on any given day.

When I was in high school, I struggled with my fashion choices. Like most teenagers, I was conscious of fitting in with my peers – fashion being the most obvious tool to do so – but I was also welcoming my newly emerging curves, which unfortunately didn't fit in with the teenage fashion trends of the 90s. As my flat-chested, narrow-hipped and spindly-legged classmates sported miniskirts, boob tubes and halter tops, I found myself floating somewhere between frantically covering my ever-increasing bust and hips with oversized jumpers, and also wanting to fit in by squeezing into questionable pieces of cloth being marketed as the latest clothing trend.

I remember one defining fashion moment that was probably the worst trend to emerge out of 1997 but served me and my chunky, short pale legs well for a period of time. It was a pair of leggings with a miniskirt attached – two items of clothing in one – which, according to Google, are called 'skirted leggings'. Anyway, in 1997 they were outrageously cool! Everyone had a pair (I believe I had two), and I remember feeling for the first time that I could finally feel fashionable as our Year Eight dance approached. But by the time the dance arrived, the trend had already passed and 70s glomesh halter tops were having a revival.

My buxom chest didn't stand a bloody chance against the bounce of the 'Nutbush'. This is life summed up in teenage fashion. It moves fast and, if you don't know who you are (who does at that age?), your identity can get pummelled into last season quicker than a pair of skirted leggings.

When I left high school, I became a bit savvier with my clothing choices. Although I was still using clothes to cover myself up, I discovered that a long, flowy maxi skirt was a feminine and fashion-forward means to mask the parts of my body that I didn't want on display. What started with a white, tiered hippie maxi skirt with broderie-anglaise trimming from a flea market slowly became my entire aesthetic. I never intended to become that boho chic, flea-market scouting, 18-year-old 'free spirit', but once my wardrobe started to lean that way, people treated me as such – a mung-bean-loving, free-love-spruiking, incense-burning, Fleetwood-Mac-listening 70s love child – and, before I knew it, my lifestyle began to follow suit.

I experimented with vegetarianism (and failed miserably), I dug my crystals out of boxes I had stored at Mum's place, I listened to Neil Young, Rodriguez and Creedence Clearwater Revival on repeat, I began to style my home with crochet throws and embellished pillows, and I even dated a stoner just to give it that real authentic flavour. Don't get me wrong, it was all genuine – I wasn't falsifying this version of me – but I would be ignorant to think that my fashion choices hadn't influenced who I identified as at that age. This was probably my first taste of breaking away from the mainstream. It was less about fitting in with my peers and more about belonging to a stylish subset. I felt for the very first time in my life that I was able to express parts of myself that I'd never fully explored before, even if it was subconsciously dictated by the clothes I wore.

By 2005, at the age of 21, my love-child aesthetic had been adopted by fast-fashion brands and high-end labels. The appeal of market bargains was not only gone, but the stall owners jacked up their prices to match the high-end retail stores. It became hard to distinguish between a genuine vintage find and a $20 knock-off, and the whole aesthetic lost its appeal. While I still continued with my love of 70s rock and had built an enviable crystal collection, I'd dropped my stoner lover and moved on to a Taurean surfer whose social group was part of the hipster fashion crowd of Sydney's eastern suburbs.

Once again, I felt like an outsider. What you wore mattered, what mattered even more was the label on those clothes and it was the first time I'd understood that the amount of money you spent on a pair of jeans gave you a prestige that just wasn't for sale in the likes of Just Jeans. Speaking of jeans, this was also the year that skinny jeans became THE jean to own in every colour. I, however, did not have the correct body type to rock a skinny jean. My legs were short, stocky and the perfect shape for straight-leg, boot-cut or boyfriend jeans, but these were not in fashion. I repeat, a fashion faux pas! Dare someone dress in a way that suited their body shape at the age of 21. What blasphemy to have that amount of autonomy in your fashion choices. So I squeezed myself (literally) into skinny jeans, feeling self-conscious every time I went out and had to stand next to my boyfriend's mates and their long-limbed, model-esque girlfriends. At the time, I felt like I didn't fit in because my body shape and the clothes that adorned it were not in vogue, but what I realise now is that when fashion changed to a style that didn't make me feel confident and cool, I completely lost sense of who the fuck I was.

By 2009, I'd been working in publishing for a couple of years and had found my groove with office attire. Even though I didn't work in fashion magazines, the queue for the lift every morning at Australia's largest magazine publisher was a real-time glimpse into what clothes were adorning the glossies that month, and I soon found a boho-meets-corporate style for myself.

Like most people starting out in a new career, I felt like an imposter most days at work. My fashion choices made me feel like I could step into the role of journalist, food writer and marketing whiz more than perhaps I believed I was worthy of. I discovered how a blazer changed not just how I showed up but also how people treated and responded to me (whether they were conscious of it or not). I wore heels on the days I wanted to dominate and feel powerful and ballet flats on the days I wanted to convey a facade of comfortable chic (or had to traipse around the CBD as a lackey for a senior member of staff).

As observers of fashion, you can see the impact that a uniform has on our perception of authority or simply recognition of someone's position. Everything from the respect a policeman's uniform demands to a simple black-and-white uniform of hospitality staff. It becomes our means to identify them, but we do this sans uniform too. The clothes we wear to any other job do exactly the same thing; they demand how one should perceive and treat you, but also how you choose to show up.

When I reached my 30s, I finally started to figure out that dressing in clothes that suited my body type was always 1000 per cent more glamorous, sexy, cute and, of course, flattering than wearing something simply because everyone else was. Not a revolutionary revelation. Why do we resist it so much growing up? The desire to 'fit in' trumps finding clothes that we actually fit in. Is it part of maturing into an adult? Or is it part of discovering our own identity free of trends and must-have lists? I finally figured out that when I feel good in my clothes, it's reflected in my attitude that day and I wear the clothes rather than the clothes wearing me.

These days, my style is simple. I have a few key pieces of clothing that are my staples and they're designated to certain occasions. But no matter how many go-to outfits you have, how many fashion trends you follow and how much money you invest in each piece, you're still going to have those days when nothing looks good. The outfit that made you feel incredible last week might now make you feel frumpy and undesirable. Did the clothes change? No mate, you did! Which brings me to my closing point, my climactic finish, my moment to shine …

Who you show up as every day has zero to do with the clothes you sport. Damn! If you're having a shit day, it's going to show no matter what you're wearing. I say this to those people (and me) who feel they are a slave to clothing choices, never feel good enough in what they wear (me, circa 2005) and struggle to 'fit in', may I be so bold as to say that it's got nothing to do with the outfit. Think of the most confident, radiant, fun, brilliant friend you have. Okay, now pop them in a hessian sack and a pair of Crocs. Still pretty bloody brilliant, aren't they? Okay, see ya! Off to burn all my clothes and cut some armholes into a couple of potato sacks.

So, what have we learned? We're told to never judge a book by its cover, yet we almost always make judgements of a person, whether it's conscious or subconscious, based on the clothes they wear (but also books, we totally judge books by their covers too). It gives us a quick flicker into who this person could be before a word is uttered. Is it an accurate system? Hell no! Is it an unfair means to identify someone? Absolutely. Do we all do it? You betcha! As fun as fashion is, it can also be a divisive system. It can segregate us by class, gender, age, race, culture and, in some instances, religion, but as limiting as that can feel at times, it's also a wonderful tool of empowerment and an incredible way to reflect to the outside world who you are on the inside. Clothes are an accessible way to express yourself, but there's a caveat: you have to be the embodiment of what you're putting out there, otherwise it's just a fashion facade. Self-awareness is knowing that wearing a power suit might give you the confidence to lead a boardroom of people, but you have to take responsibility for what happens next. What's more important than the item of clothing itself is how the item of clothing makes you feel.

Exercise 2
LET'S TAKE A TRIP DOWN FASHION MEMORY LANE

This exercise is meant to be a bit of fun. If fashion is not, and has never been, your thing, humour me by doing this exercise anyway. The fact that you don't care about what you wear might be just as revealing as if you do.

Get out your self-awareness journal and answer the following questions:

1. Do I enjoy choosing what clothes to wear?

2. How have my fashion choices changed over the years?

3. Do different clothing choices reflect the mood that I'm in?

4. Have I ever used fashion as a means of fitting in?

5. Do I use fashion as a way to portray who I am to others?

6. If I had to describe my fashion sense now, what would it be?

7. If I had one outfit in my wardrobe to reflect who I am at my essence, what would it be?

Again, there are no right or wrong answers here. I'm simply asking you to get curious about what role your clothing choices, past and present, have made on your sense of identity.

There are so many different ways in which we superficially choose to identify ourselves: relationships, social status, geography, possessions, the list goes on and on, and while I won't go into all of them in depth, I think there is one more that we do need to highlight, mostly because it's the one I still struggle to separate myself from – career. Have you ever felt that your role at work is how you define yourself, even when office hours are over? I know I have (and often still do). Let's have a look at the impact your job title has on your identity, and why my personal résumé is rather complicated.

Multiple personalities

'What do you do?' It's a foolproof icebreaker. That was until it became woke to not ask people what they do and instead ask them what lights them up, who they want to be or what they're passionate about. I mean, all that stuff's great, but like, I can make so many more assumptions about you based on your job title, ya know? You're a lawyer. You work in an office. You wear a suit most days. You likely go out of your way not to break the law. I assume you make decent money. You probably work longer hours than you'd like. I'm guessing you have a five-year plan? Now, you and I both know that's not enough information to really know who someone is, yet I have chosen to identify myself by the work I do for as long as I can remember.

In my case, it poses a wee problem … you see, I don't have just one job title. I never have, as I've always dipped my fingers into all of the honey pots. I'm a writer but also a yoga teacher. I'm a podcast host but also the editor, producer and writer of said podcast. I'm a trained chef, recipe developer and spent a good chunk of my career as a journalist. I'm not bragging, I'm just confessing that if I choose to identify myself by my profession(s), I don't know who the fuck I am. My identity is wrapped up in myriad different skill sets, uniforms and bios. I transcend different genres, categories and occupation options on official forms. When I have to go through customs and list just one occupation, the one I pick is always very telling of my mood that day.

Today, I'll be a writer! I'll walk with the swagger of a writer and I might even put a pen through my bun, even though I rarely write with a pen (or wear my hair in a bun). 'Writer' feels like a title I can be proud of. I use it to impress. Does it work? Who the fuck knows? What I do know is that it makes *me* feel something and in that transformation, the energy of the conversation changes.

But on other days in other crowds when I'm in another mood, I like to say I'm a yoga teacher. It gives people the impression that I'm grounded, flexible and at peace with my own demons. (FYI, most yoga teachers aren't. It's a little trick we like to play called, 'If I talk nice and slow, you'll believe I've got my shit together.' I say this because I am a master at it.) Every now and then, I'll be a chef. Not when I'm around other chefs or even competent home cooks but when I'm in a group of people who look like they could barely toast bread. Yes, that's the kind of crowd where I will happily dish out kitchen hacks and unique flavour combinations while people ooh and aah in awe.

We are a society of labels. We label ourselves and we label others. We make assumptions about lawyers' five-year plans, waiters having side hustles, folks on TV living their dream and bartenders being transient. We label accountants as boring, musicians as troubled and chefs as aggressive. I've listed stereo-types but what I've come to realise is that what I do to my own identity is far more detrimental than reinforcing or even debunking a few stereotypes. I use my career as a lazy way of explaining who I am and to bolster my personality. My role as a published author makes me sound way more impressive than if I omitted this information but what I've realised is that if my career defines my personality, then I am dealing with multiple personalities. If all my jobs were taken from me overnight, which truth be told happened to many of us during the pandemic, who would I be then?

Now, you might not have several jobs like me. You might just have one very clear job or perhaps you don't work in a classic career and rather as a parent, carer or volunteer. Regardless, I urge you to get curious about whether you use your job title as a means of identification, and if it no longer existed, what would you be left with? I can't believe I'm about to make another *Friends* reference so early on in this book but I have a mate who is very much like Chandler Bing in the sense that no one has any idea what he does for a living.

We've been friends since we were 16, he is married to another one of my best friends and still I have absolutely no idea what happens to him between 9am and 5pm every day (he's definitely not a transponster, I know that much!). I know it's important and I know that he is integral to whatever goes on at his work-place, but aside from that, he's just our mate Fred*. Whatever goes on at that office is not how he defines his relationship as a husband, father, friend or son. His job title doesn't carry his personality or the way he chooses to communicate with others because we have no bloody idea what he does for work and we choose to love him anyway. I use this example not to illustrate that we should never bring work home, talk about what we do or celebrate our work successes but rather to point out that you must be able to express yourself from what's going on inside of you rather than external factors that could disappear at any moment.

I have another mate, Ellie*, who worked in events management. She ran lots of different types of events – music festivals, product launches, food shows and corporate symposiums – you name it, her team were behind the scenes making sure that every event was executed seamlessly. That job was her life because it took up most of her time and she was wildly passionate about it but also because she used it to define her worth. When the pandemic hit in early 2020, her business became not only redundant, because events were banned, but it also became completely unviable and she eventually had to close it down.

Ellie, like many people who lost their businesses that year, had to not only find an alternate income stream but she also found herself in the middle of an identity crisis. How was she to celebrate her successes, chart her failures and measure her self-worth if not by the business she'd put her everything into? She was a mess, and understandably! Ellie and I had lots of late-night (wine-fuelled) Zoom conversations about this. I would be exactly the same if I was stripped of all my job titles. In conversations with my friends who left their careers to become stay-at-home parents, they too speak of an identity crisis that strikes when they're no longer doing the thing they had once so ruthlessly defined themselves by. So what about you? Do you define yourself by the work you do?

Exercise 3
WHO ARE YOU WITHOUT YOUR JOB?

This exercise is about contemplating how much weight you give your job title when it comes to defining who you are. No judgement here – as I said, I invest way too much of my identity in the fact that I'm a published author. The point of this exercise (and the two that preceded it) is for you to get clear on how you identify now, so that once we start shining a light on who you really are, you'll notice that you're ten times more impressive than you thought you were!

Answer the following questions:

1. What's my job title?

2. Do I lead with this in small-talk conversations?

3. Do I find myself making assumptions about other people based on their job title?

4. Do I think my work makes me sound more interesting?

5. If I were stripped of my job title and work achievements today, how would I feel?

I am by no means asking you to care less or not find passion in your career. I just want you to be able to separate your identity from what you do for work. The same goes for your physical appearance, fashion choices, relationships, home, social status, geographical location, etc. You can still enjoy all of those things (no one can make me give up my penchant for winter coats) but what's important is that you're a whole person without them. Make sense?

Over one of our late-night conversations, I asked Ellie if she'd be open to letting me help her rediscover herself. She was keen, and I hope you are too – because that's where we're now headed. It's time to get curious about who you are without all that stuff!

LET'S GO INWARD

There are several things that go into defining your identity and this book is designed to help you have a better grasp of who you are in your entirety. When combined, the six aspects of self-awareness will give you a fabulous overview of self but it's also important to be aware that you're constantly evolving with every new experience, circumstance, person and hurdle you encounter in your life. My hope with this book is that you leave with a beautiful blueprint of who you are and that you keep adding to it (or taking away) as you grow and mature throughout your life. This is why I must reiterate that self-awareness is a lifelong practice.

In the rest of this chapter on identity, we will be focusing on who you are at a vibrational level, what your personal core values are in life, and what strengths and weaknesses make up your personality and govern your energy as a foundation for everything that is to come in the following chapters. Sound good?!

Discovering your personal vibration

So, back to my friend Ellie. She closed down her events management business after major events were cancelled and brands were unwilling to schedule anything for the future due to the massive uncertainty of COVID-19. After spending months trying to stay afloat and look after her staff, Ellie decided the most sensible way forward was to close down the business completely and pivot.

Enter Ellie's major identity crisis. Who was she without the title of Badass Boss Lady? What was she passionate about if it wasn't the brands that she dedicated her life to and the events she poured her heart and soul into? Also, and I quote, 'Jord, I am nothing without my business! I don't even know what I like to do for fun!' Ellie is an extreme example but I think to some degree we can all relate to leaning into the external – such as our work, clothing choices, relationships, political ideology, social circles and the suburb we live in – to define what lights us up, brings us joy and illuminates our eccentricities and quirks.

If you've read my book *Higher Love*, you'll be familiar with the concept of your personal vibration in relation to manifesting love in your life. But, the thing is, your personal vibration is capable of attracting so much more than that. In fact, it is responsible for manifesting everything in your life – opportunities, experiences, people, EVERYTHING – which we can agree is great! But what the heck is it?

Well, in its simplest form, your personal vibration is your authenticity; it's a frequency emitted from you when you are being 100 per cent true to yourself. There is no prescription or formula for authenticity, which makes it irritating when people tell you to 'just be your authentic self' as if it's something you innately know how to be. Authenticity is defined as being real or true, but in order to be true to yourself or be the real you, you have to know yourself, acknowledge yourself, accept yourself and express yourself, which all require an acute sense of self-awareness. You know when I said earlier that you manifest who you are? Well, I was referring to your personal vibration – the frequency that makes you uniquely you. Once you're familiar with it, you have the ability to strengthen it or weaken it.

When it's strong, that's when you attract incredible things into your life with very little effort (aka easeful manifestation).

Exercise 4

GETTING CURIOUS ABOUT YOUR PERSONAL VIBRATION

Set aside 10–15 minutes to do this exercise. Free yourself from distractions, get nice and comfortable, dim the lights if possible and limit the amount of sound around you.

Lie down or sit comfortably – all that matters is that you feel at ease. Now, close your eyes and recall when in your life you feel most like yourself. It could be around certain people or in certain environments. It could be a specific situation you've experienced or a particular activity that you do. For me, it's when I'm around certain friends or when I'm on my own in nature. In these moments, I feel like I can be 100 per cent me.

Indicators to look for when you feel most like yourself include:

(You feel comfortable in your body.

(Words flow and conversation is easeful.

(You're not second-guessing yourself or those around you.

(You feel safe and confident.

When you pinpoint the moments that you feel like your most authentic self, ask yourself:

❨ How do I feel in my body?

❨ What's my posture like?

❨ What emotions come easily to me?

❨ How do I communicate?

❨ What stands out about myself when I feel most like me?

Realising that all of your reflections above are wonderful indicators that your personal vibration is strong and that you are in alignment with your authenticity can be so illuminating when it comes to understanding yourself better. It's so useful to be aware of what strengthens your personal vibration when you can feel it begin to weaken (i.e. when you feel unable to be yourself).

Now, consider when in your life you find it difficult to connect with your most authentic self. You know what I'm talking about – when you're in certain situations or around particular people and it feels near impossible to be 100 per cent you.

Indicators to look for when you feel like you can't be yourself may include:

❨ You feel uncomfortable in your body.

❨ You stumble on your words or struggle to contribute to conversation.

❨ You second-guess yourself and those around you constantly.

❨ You feel unsafe and unconfident.

A weakened personal vibration will manifest differently for everyone, but I know that mine is weak when I struggle to contribute to conversation, my posture slumps, my witty one-liners are nowhere to be found and my energy drains from my body. It's important to recognise that a weakened vibration is not the same as being fearful of trying something new or simply being in an unfamiliar environment. There is a subtle difference, and the more you know what a strong personal vibration feels like, the more you will notice when it is being compromised.

Can you pinpoint the moments in your life when you feel like your vibration has been compromised? Ask yourself:

❨ How do I feel in my body?

❨ What happens to my posture?

❨ What emotions do I feel?

❨ How's my communication affected?

❨ Does anything else about myself stand out when I find it difficult to access my most authentic self?

Now, draw a line down the centre of a page in your self-awareness journal. On one side of the page write 'strengthens'. On the other side write 'weakens'. You might be able to fill in both columns straight away, knowing what things strengthen your vibration (i.e. when you feel like the truest and best version of yourself) and when your vibration feels weakened or compromised. As we move through each aspect of self-awareness, you will discover more and more things to add to both sides of the list. I encourage you to do this.

My dear old friend Ellie and I surmised that everything that strengthened her vibration in the previous exercise was all work related, and when it was all taken away, it left her in a weakened personal vibration and out of alignment with the kick-ass Ellie I know and love outside of her work. For you, it might not be work. It might be that your identity is wrapped up in what you look like, how disciplined your yoga practice is, what kind of a parent you are, what political party you support or how many followers you have on Instagram. Perhaps your identity isn't wrapped up in any of those things either, or you've never even stopped to consider who you are. That's cool too. Either way, we've got work to do.

Your valuable assets

When I asked Ellie what her values were, she started rattling off the mission statement of her (former) business – which we giggled at – but we also recognised that Ellie was the core of her business so she wasn't too far off. What she needed to get super clear on, however, was what her core values were so that she could use them as her own personal guidance system to determine whether something (or someone) was in alignment with who she truly was.

Think of your values as the core of your identity. They give you a clear and tangible framework for how you live your life so that you can stand confidently in the truth of who you are and strengthen your personal vibration. When your values are compromised, it can throw off your alignment, which in turn pulls you out of your authenticity and has you questioning your identity. How cool is it to have a barometer of sorts that can warn you of this before it's too late? That's what your values are, my friend – your own internal barometer.

When I first sat down to determine my personal core values, I struggled big time to come up with any. I wanted to google 'what are good values to have?', worried that whatever I concocted on my own wouldn't be enough. The turning point for me when determining my values was realising that they were simply feelings that I value in my life. If you've read *Make It Happen*, you'll be aware what a profound impact our feelings have on our vibrational energy, so it makes sense that when we're aligned with the feelings that feel good, we're strengthening our vibration and when we're in situations that don't allow us to access those feelings (or values), our vibration is weakened.

Exercise 5

DISCOVERING YOUR
PERSONAL CORE VALUES

We've determined that an easy way to figure out your values is by looking at them as feelings you desire to experience in your life. Another way to look at it is to define what feelings mean the most to you.

What feelings are important and necessary for you to be fulfilled in life? List the feelings that you value as core parts of your vibration.

If you struggle to determine what these are, think of different times in your life when you felt really bloody good. When you've identified one of these scenarios, really feel into that moment and ask yourself: what feelings did I access in that moment? Get curious and keep digging until you uncover every feeling.

Next, I want you to ask yourself: are there feelings I long to experience in my life that are important to me but perhaps I haven't experienced yet? Or have I felt the opposite of those feelings, which made me realise why it's so important to experience the feelings I desire? These can also be added to your list.

If you're looking for a little inspiration, you will find a list of feelings to prompt your values at https://www.jordannalevin.com/make-you-happen-downloads. Choosing the top five feelings that you desire in your life is a good start. Of course, you may desire feelings that are not on this list and that is absolutely fine. You may also have more than five core values, but I have found in the past that when you have a long list of core values, they start to become diluted. Start with five and then work up from there, practising the art of staying in alignment with them along the way.

If you're still unsure, start a sentence with 'I feel ...' and then insert each word from the list of feelings, and notice which ones connect with you.

So, you've determined what your personal core values are by looking at them as feelings you desire to experience. But how does one put these values to use, you might ask? The simplest method I've found is whenever you're in a situation where you're unsure whether it's uncertainty about a decision, discomfort in your environment or a moment where your authenticity needs to take the lead, ask yourself: am I able to access my core values in this situation? Can I feel the way I desire or am I actually feeling the opposite? If you can't access it or you're feeling the opposite, it's a pretty good indicator that you're compromising on a value or that you're not in full alignment with your authenticity. And yes, of course, we can't be in alignment with our values all of the time but golly gosh it's helpful to have something to aim for so you're not compromising on them left, right and centre simply because you never took the time to get clear on what they are.

Ellie's personal core values were freedom, independence, honesty, creativity and integrity. She discovered that those values applied to all areas of her life: relationships, career, finances, social life, family and wellbeing. You might find that different values relate to certain areas of your life but not to others. That's totally fine. All I want is for you to get curious, which, as luck would have it, is the first of the three steps to self-awareness. Actually, this is the perfect time to show you how you can apply the three steps of self-awareness. I'll use myself as an example.

One of my personal core values is safety. I know, super sexy. I use it as a pick-up line at singles nights. (Jokes, I don't go to singles nights.) It's taken me three decades to acknowledge that safety is a vital part of my personal vibration. Let me show you how I got there (hopefully you won't need three decades because you have this handy three-step process).

Step 1: Curiosity

When I first decided to identify my personal core values, I did exactly what I instructed you to do in Exercise 5: I recalled situations in my life where I was able to be myself and, in turn, be fully seen for who I truly was. I realised it was always in a situation where I felt safe. Physically, yes – I've never felt like myself when dangling from a high-rise building (FYI I've never done this, but it's a safe bet that I wouldn't feel safe) – but more so in terms of feeling supported and secure in my choices, ideas and words, and also notably safe in the environment or around the people I was with. If I hadn't done that exercise and viewed my values as feelings, I don't think I would have ever realised that safety was a major personal core value of mine. This is why self-enquiry and self-reflection are so important. We must set aside the time to get curious or, chances are, we won't.

HOT TIP: It's good to be aware that your values will shift and change as you continue to experience life. When it comes to being self-aware, never stop questioning your values and what keeps you aligned with them.

Step 2: Acceptance

When I truly contemplated my personal core values, I kept avoiding writing down 'safety'. Mostly because, as we've already established, it's not the sexiest of values but once I was able to accept that – sexy or not – safety was super important to me, then I was able to make changes in my life to reflect that. When it comes to accepting your values, I recommend the following:

★ Recognise the importance of a particular core value to you and your personal vibration.
★ Acknowledge the significance of remaining true to your

value. What will it enable you to do? For example, when I feel safe, it allows me to be more vulnerable and take more risks.

★ It's also helpful to recognise what you sacrifice in order to stay true to your values. It can be challenging to remain true to ourselves at all times – if it was easy, we'd be living in an entirely different world. There are times when I test my limits with my own safety, such as whether this person I'm dating makes me feel safe enough to relax into who I truly am. If not, then my value, but also my sense of identity, is immediately compromised.

★ Embracing and accepting your values allows you to strengthen your vibration simply by being you. It's as simple as that.

Step 3: Embodiment

When it comes to embodying a value, I ask myself: how is my value of safety being reflected in my actions and behaviours? Do I put myself in situations that honour my value or compromise it? Because I value safety so highly, I ensure the safety of others, not just myself. I also create healthy boundaries that allow me to feel safe in certain environments or around certain people. The key to embodying a value is to walk the talk and be the living and breathing personification of that value. If you value honesty, then ask yourself: am I being honest with myself and others? If creativity is one of your values, then ask yourself: how can I inject creativity into this situation? You get the picture. You have to *be* your values, express your values and make sure that your actions and behaviours are a reflection of your core personal values. This is what keeps us aligned and authentic.

Your sparkling personality

I am fascinated by the intricacies of people's personalities, especially the quirks that lie beneath a sunny disposition. I used to think it was just my penchant for dark streaks in unavailable men but on further analysis, I decided that I'm drawn to the less sunny side of people's personalities because I feel it allows me to see the real them. That's not to say there's not authenticity in our lighter sides but a robust personality will embrace and express both light and shade in equal measure and I encourage you to do the same. Have you ever taken the time to get curious about your own personality and what has contributed to it to make you who you are? While there are certain attributes and qualities that you're born with, your environment, parenting, societal variables and even astrology are also major contributing factors. We are a melting pot of our own experiences, and I don't know about you but I've felt parts of my personality change as I've matured, grown wiser and started to give less fucks.

There are so many ways to analyse personality types. Hippocrates suggests that there are four fundamental personality types: sanguine (pleasure-seeking and sociable), choleric (ambitious and leader-like), melancholic (analytical and literal) and phlegmatic (relaxed and thoughtful). If you've ever done a Myers Briggs personality test you'll be familiar with psychoanalyst Carl Jung's personality types theory, as his teachings are the inspiration for this test. Jung's theory uses four psychological functions:

thinking and feeling (rational functions) as well as sensation and intuition (irrational functions). In addition, he distinguishes between two fundamental life attitudes: introversion and extra-version. And we can't really talk about famous psychoanalysts' theories without discussing Sigmund Freud, who suggested that our behaviours and personality are driven by our innate drives and needs. There are a multitude of personality tests you can do online to gain insight into your own mix of qualities and attributes, including 'What is my spirit animal?' and 'Are you a Rachel or a Monica?' (I knew I could squeeze in one more *Friends* reference!), or if you're actually looking for something helpful, I highly recommend the Myers Briggs test. But, in saying that, I do believe that the more you progress through this book and do the exercises I've laid out for you, the more you will gain a better understanding of your own unique personality – something a multiple-choice test online could never accurately divulge.

As we move forward, we're going to look less at personality types and more at personality traits. Something to note is that a personality trait only becomes synonymous with you when you're consistent with it. For example, it would be inaccurate for me to call myself a patient person because of that one time I waited for my soup to cool without shovelling it into my mouth when my history of soup sipping shows a track record of me burning my mouth because I can't wait for the temperature to drop.

Together, we're going to look at some basic personality traits that you might possess. Not all of them are going to be positive but that's the point of this next exercise. It's about you recognising that you may have a few less-than-positive personality traits included in the mix of what makes you who you are. I'm hesitant to call them negative because I feel like, again, back to the Law of Polarity, the negative traits are needed to contribute to the whole (i.e. you), and a simple awareness of your less-positive traits (or weaknesses) inevitably becomes your strength. But for argument's sake, I've included positive, neutral and negative personality traits. The following exercise invites you to get curious. That's all I want you to think about for now – getting inquisitive about your personality. No judgement, no guilt, just pure curiosity.

Exercise 6
PERSONALITY PICKER

There are two ways you can tackle this exercise:

1. Grab your self-awareness journal and write down the personality traits you identify with.

2. I've created a PDF of different personality traits that you can find here: https://www.jordannalevin.com/make-you-happen-downloads. You can print out the PDF and tick off the personality traits you possess (although, keep in mind that these might shift and change over time).

I've concocted a beautiful mix of positive, neutral and 'negative' personality traits. Choose the ones that are MOST prominent for you (I've probably exhibited the majority of the traits at some point in my life, but we're looking for consistency here, folks).

If you're still not sure, contemplate the following for some inspiration:

- ❨ How do I deal with stressful situations?

- ❨ How would my friends describe me?

- ❨ How do I react when faced with a decision?

- ❨ When I need to finish a task, what's my approach?

- ❨ When I care about a cause, what do I do?

- ❨ How do I deal with a deadline?

- ❨ What's my process around creative projects?

- ❨ I've just been entrusted with top secret information – what do I do?

- ❨ What's my approach when planning a birthday party or overseas holiday?

- ❨ What kind of advice do I give?

- ❨ What are my natural talents?

Reminder: There's no judgement here, so be as honest as you can with yourself. This is a means of getting to know yourself better, not a means to berate, condemn or be ashamed of yourself. In fact, I want you to celebrate yourself, knowing that your shadow side is what makes your light side so bloody bright and brilliant.

If you've never done work like this before, it can be a lot to take in all at once. There's no rush to comprehend it fully; just be open to the process. What I want you to take away from this is that your personal vibration is the essence of who you are, and when you can identify with your own authentic expression, there is less of a need to grasp onto skirted leggings, impressive job titles or a certain body weight. Whenever my life feels seemingly out of my control, I feel overwhelmed by indecision or I feel helpless within my circumstances, I always come back to my personal vibration. I notice how I feel in my body and the qualities in my personality that emerge when I am in a low vibration, and then I do more of the things that I know will strengthen my vibration to bring me back into alignment with who I really am. This is why I got you to write that list. Refer to the 'strengthens' column whenever you need inspiration to do the things that will remind you of who you are.

As we move through each aspect of self and apply the three steps of self-awareness along the way, your personal vibration will naturally strengthen. As we identify your weaknesses in certain aspects and how to turn them into assets, your vibration will strengthen. As you learn about boundaries and how to trust yourself like never before, your vibration will strengthen. And lastly, by releasing limiting beliefs and creating new rewarding ones, you guessed it, your vibration will strengthen.

Being aware of your personal vibration at its strongest doesn't mean anything less is a weaker you or a less-than-perfect you, because perfect should never be the goal. Having an acute sense of your personal vibration is simply a barometer for your potential and an accurate way to access your true identity. Once you have an awareness of your potential, then you will naturally attract, align with and feel worthy of anything you want to create in your life. This, my friend, is what it means to manifest who you are.

A LITTLE BIT ABOUT ME

After reading through the first aspect of self – identity – and doing all of the exercises that invited you to get curious about your identity, write one paragraph describing who you are without using your work, wardrobe, relationships, material possessions, etc. to define you.

Some tips for writing:

  ❨ Concentrate on your personal core values and personality traits.

  ❨ Use positive and empowering language.

  ❨ Write it in the present tense. A great way to start is with the statement, 'I am ...'

As we progress through each aspect of self-awareness in this book, you'll notice how much more you'll be able to enrich this paragraph with the wonderful things you learn about yourself along the way.

IDENTITY AND THE THREE STEPS OF SELF-AWARENESS

At the end of each aspect, you're going to take everything you've learned and apply the three steps of self-awareness to it. This isn't an exercise that you do in your journal and then that's that. Oh no, this is something that you integrate into your life and practise every day. Don't let that stress you out, let it excite you! This book isn't a guide to being a better person, it's a book about getting to know who you are. Period. From this space, wondrous things become possible. Trust that.

Step 1: Curiosity

You've spent this entire chapter getting curious about your identity. If you've skipped over the exercises, you're forgiven (this one time), but until you've taken the time to do them, then you're no closer to being self-aware than when you first picked up this book. So please go back and complete them before moving forward and remind yourself that you're discovering who you are so that you can increase your ability to manifest anything you desire. If you're looking for some extracurricular lines of enquiry around identity, you might like to look into the following:

★ Does your identity shift in different situations? For example, is it different at work than at home? If this is the case, that's totally fine and normal – just something to be conscious of. Are you remaining true to yourself in both situations?
★ Are there times when you abandon your identity? Can you see a common thread behind why?

Step 2: Acceptance

Self-acceptance is the practice of accepting one's whole self – light and shade, strengths and weaknesses, potentials and limitations, talents and shortcomings. Here are some pointers to consider:

- ★ Did you find that there were superficial factors that shaped your identity? Can you accept that it's beneficial to have acknowledged that rather than deny that it was ever the case?
- ★ Can you acknowledge the importance of staying true to your core values for the sake of your personal vibration?
- ★ When looking at your personality traits, were there truths uncovered that you likely dismissed or chose to ignore?

Remember, the first part of acceptance is acknowledging who you are – strengths AND weaknesses – and recognising that together they make you who you are.

Step 3: Embodiment

This is the fun bit! You have a whole new perspective on who you are, and it's time to share it with the world. Here are some things to consider when it comes to embodying your identity:

- ★ Now that you're aware of who you are on the inside and what a strong personal vibration feels like, how can you start to reflect that in the way you dress, the way you communicate and how you show up as a friend, lover, employee and/or boss?
- ★ Now that you have clarity of what your personal core values are, how can you be a living and breathing example of them? Write down some ideas in your self-awareness journal if you think it will help.

★ Now that you understand your personality better than ever, how can you embrace all facets of who you are? Instead of using certain traits as an excuse, how can you turn them into strengths?

★ Can you consciously alter your actions and behaviours to support your values and personality traits?

You probably found that, as you made your way through this rather meaty chapter, much of the external things that you identify with do wholeheartedly shape who you are on the inside – that's beautiful. Your culture, religious beliefs, childhood experiences, geographical location and penchant for sequins and winged eyeliner will all have an impact on your personal vibration, values and personality, but it's important that you're also able to separate yourself from those things so that you don't mistake those external factors for who you truly are at your essence. Make sense? Great, let's proceed ...

CHAPTER 4

Emotions

In Season Three of *Grey's Anatomy*, Meredith Grey dies. Except she doesn't, because the show is up to its 18th season and Ellen Pompeo's character is still well and truly alive. Yet, I still mourn her death. I cry actual tears, sobbing uncontrollably into a box of tissues. The feeling of loss is visceral. It's as if my own friend had just drowned and couldn't be saved.

It's always fascinated me that our emotions can't decipher between what's real and what's not. In fact, I find it easier to cry over things that aren't real than things that are. For example, take the death of my family dog. After 16 years of loving this dog unconditionally, he passed away at the most inconvenient time. I was 24 hours away from a visit to my family farm – which was a 900-kilometre drive away – and he couldn't wait just one more day for me to say goodbye.

I was so incredibly devastated. I felt sad to lose a beloved family member, guilt for not getting down there sooner and anger because, well, the whole thing was just bloody unfair! I didn't cry, though. I didn't yell. I didn't even get that sinking feeling that guilt sometimes elicits. I had to scroll through photos of him to try and summon some sort of physical reaction that indicated sadness. I was aiming for tears – the kind I shed for Meredith Grey – but they didn't come.

Am I a sociopath? I pondered to myself one afternoon. Surely not! I'd always thought I was quite a sensitive person. I often find myself distraught while watching movies about animals or too easily offended when someone yells at me when I'm driving. But why is it that when the pain is so close to home that I find it hard to just let the tears gush out of me? 'Too much skin in the game,' a wise and emotionally intelligent gal pal once said to me. 'You think you're super in touch with your feelings but you're bypassing them by thinking about them and labelling them without allowing yourself to actually physically process them.'

Hmm, she's not wrong. I would much rather rationalise, analyse and overthink an emotion than feel it in my body. It seems like a waste of time and unproductive. And you know what? Emotions can really fucking hurt sometimes, especially ones like grief, fear and anger. Realising that I think my feelings rather than feel them was a life-changing revelation, mostly because it became apparent that thinking my feelings was going to fuck with my manifestation efforts big time.

WHY EMOTIONS ARE INTEGRAL TO MANIFESTATION

If you've read *Make It Happen* and you're familiar with the Manifestation Equation, you'll know that feelings are one of the four integral components of manifesting successfully. Your feelings (or emotions) are energy in motion and they're responsible for supercharging your vibrational frequency, so it's imperative that you're feeling them and not suppressing, ignoring or bypassing them because that's going to block your ability to manifest. Alternatively, maybe you have so many emotions that you don't know what to do with them – they pour out of you like an endless stream and it's hard to sort through what's what and which emotion belongs where.

This isn't good either, because your feelings become intertwined and lack clarity, which makes it difficult to direct your energy with the precision required to manifest. Or perhaps you're like me and intellectualise your emotions – convincing yourself that you're emotionally savvy – but in essence you're just sorting and rationalising feelings and doing nothing to embody them, which means you're not getting any of the vibrational benefits and your manifestations are affected. My point is that we're all emotionally wired differently. One emotional type is not necessarily better than the other and you're not necessarily emoting incorrectly. Being aware of your unique emotional process can not only be illuminating for you to get to know yourself better, but it will also enable you to improve and fine-tune your manifestation practice. So, that's what we're going to explore in this chapter. You're going to become intimately aware of your emotional self, because here's the thing: if you can't recognise how you feel an emotion, process it and express it, you're going to stunt your ability to manifest with ease and ain't nobody got time for that!

THE EMOTIONAL TYPES

It took me the better part of three decades to realise that emotions are not felt, processed and expressed in the same way for everyone. When I found myself frustrated with ex-boyfriends and their inability to communicate how they were feeling, it was unfair of me to yell expletives at them and make wildly unfounded assumptions that they didn't love me simply because they had trouble expressing it. When girlfriends broke down in tears after I gave them a bite of my truth sandwich or dished up some helpful criticism, it wasn't okay for me to label them as oversensitive and pity their emotional instability. And when I'd received upsetting news and knew that I was sad, could communicate how sad I was but struggled to cry (sometimes, not all the time), it didn't mean I was a sociopath, it just meant that I experienced my emotions differently. I found that once I was able to understand my emotions better, it gave me more capacity to understand the emotions of those around me. So I committed to developing my emotional smarts.

When I was 21, I picked up a book by American psychologist Daniel Goleman titled *Emotional Intelligence*. At the time, I read it so people on the bus would think I was smarter than I was but it wasn't until I re-read it in my early 30s that the teachings finally clicked. The psychological theory of emotional intelligence was developed by Peter Salovey and John Mayer (not *that* John Mayer), who describe emotional intelligence as one's ability to perceive, use, understand, manage and handle emotions.

In Goleman's book, he outlines the five components of emotional intelligence: self-awareness, self-regulation, self-motivation, empathy and social skills. In this book, we're going to stick to the self-awareness component and get curious about how you recognise and perceive your emotions, gain clarity around your emotions, as well as process, manage and express your emotions. Because once you're able to see your emotional self in the light, you can recognise what a profound impact your emotional intelligence has not only on your thoughts, actions and manifestations, but also the way you relate, create and communicate with those around you. This makes emotional intelligence a pretty crucial skill, don't you think?

If you were in a psychology lecture, you'd likely learn that there are four different emotional types, to which I would say, 'Excuse me, lecturer – and likely expert in your field of psychology – I think you'll find there are more than four types. I've dated, befriended, worked with and served (in my days as a waitress) at least six of them.' But, since you're not here to become a psychologist and I assume you're not using my knowledge and lack of expertise to psychologically diagnose other people, I think it's safe to share my emotional types theory with you. Let's make it fun and entertaining, though, because emotions can be a real drag, am I right? If you answered yes, then it's likely that you identify with a couple of guests at the following dinner party. Picture this …

The dinner party of Ms Prettyeyes

It's a humid night in the middle of January. A summer storm is rolling in after a blistering hot day and an elaborate dinner party is planned at the pompous estate of a bestselling author who has pretty eyes and a witty disposition (it's not me, but thanks for thinking my eyes are pretty). Five guests are invited to this soiree – none of them have met prior – and they've spent the day on the grounds of the estate at the request of their hostess before being summoned for dinner in the dining hall. On arrival, they're met by the butler Jeeves (that's what all good butlers are called, right?). 'I regret to inform you that Ms Prettyeyes cannot join you for dinner tonight. There was an accident this afternoon and she has fallen to her death.'

There are gasps among the guests and pleas to know what happened. 'She tripped down the grand staircase while balancing a tray of champagne-filled flutes,' Jeeves proclaimed. 'Her last words to me were, "Make sure they enjoy the dinner party. I slaved over it all day".' There's a ruckus among the guests as they grapple with the shocking news of their hostess's unfortunate and untimely demise.

Jeeves leads them through to the dining room and each person takes a seat at the table. The guests had only ever met Ms Prettyeyes once or twice before – no one was a close friend – but each held this woman in high regard. With such shocking and devastating news being thrust upon them, each guest processes the death of their hostess in that moment very differently.

Guest 1: Ms Fountain

Ms Fountain is sobbing. She's completely overwhelmed by the news of Ms Prettyeyes's passing. She tries to speak but she is so overwhelmed by an influx of emotion that she cannot really make sense of. She just feels what she feels and loses any sense of a social filter that one might apply when seated among a group of strangers. 'It's not fair,' she wails. 'She was taken so soon.' She sobs uncontrollably into her linen napkin and wonders why the gentleman sitting next to her is showing no emotion whatsoever. She rests her head on his stiff shoulder to elicit some sympathy. Ms Fountain finds Mr Pokerface familiar, although they've never met before. He reminds her of many of the men she's dated and a little of her mother.

Guest 2: Mr Pokerface

Mr Pokerface is scared to move and disturb Ms Fountain. He can't understand why she's sobbing over a woman she's only met a couple of times before – what exactly is she so sad about? He decides to stay very still and wonders if they're serving wine at this dinner party. He asks the woman sitting on the other side of him if she'd mind passing the bread and notices that she isn't wearing a wedding ring. He'll definitely ask her for her number tonight. Did she just give him a come-hither look?

Guest 3: Ms Brainy

Ms Brainy wonders why Mr Pokerface keeps looking at her and hopes he doesn't ask her out. She too is a little confused by the waterworks flooding from Ms Fountain but can understand that the death of someone, even someone you don't know very well, is something one might be saddened by. She contemplates how she feels about the situation.

She's shocked, sympathetic for Ms Prettyeyes's loved ones and definitely a little uncomfortable about continuing to eat dinner in her house as if the woman hadn't just died THAT DAY! Also, how did this happen? When is the funeral? Was she married? She mentioned a dog the last time they spoke so who is looking after her dog? There is much to process and think about here, Ms Brainy decides, but breaking down into a blubbering mess isn't on her agenda this evening. She tries to throw Mr Pokerface off her scent and instead leans to the man on her left.

Guest 4: Mr Compassion

'Are you okay?' Mr Compassion asks Ms Brainy. 'This is all so sudden. Would you like to talk about how you're feeling?'

'I'm okay,' replies Ms Brainy. 'I've just been thinking about the absurdity of sitting at a dead woman's dining table.' Mr Compassion is worried that Ms Brainy is all up in her head. He feels deep sympathy for her obvious discomfort and at the same time extreme sadness as he witnesses Ms Fountain sobbing into her napkin.

'Will you excuse me?' he says to Ms Brainy and rushes to be beside the exploding fire hydrant on the other side of the dining table.

Let's go back briefly to Ms Brainy and Mr Pokerface ... Ms Brainy is left with her thoughts and has no choice but to talk to Mr Pokerface. 'So, how do you know Ms Prettyeyes?' she inquires. 'Is this your first time visiting the estate? How are you feeling about this weird dinner party? I'm wondering if this is all some sort of big ruse, to be honest. That's why I'm struggling to feel sad. It's almost as if I'm waiting to make sure it's real before I commit to the tears, ya know?'

Mr Pokerface didn't know. He couldn't remember the last time he felt sad. But he nodded in agreement so that Ms Brainy would continue to chat to him. She continued, 'Do you think Ms Fountain knew her better than the rest of us? Is that why she's blubbering like that? How are you feeling?' Ms Brainy waits for Mr Pokerface's response. 'Ah yeah, I'm not sure,' he responds.

'I feel fine, I guess. Honestly, I'm just glad we're here because how would I have had the pleasure of meeting you otherwise?' Ms Brainy rolls her eyes. He cannot be serious.

Guest 5: Ms Boulder

Ms Boulder has been quietly observing the room, intrigued by the diverse reactions of everyone around her. She's been practising deep belly breathing to ensure her nervous system is calm. She understands that everyone is dealing with this unusual situation in their own way and wonders if she can be of assistance to the other guests.

She starts with Mr Pokerface. 'How are you coping with this unusual evening?' she inquires. 'I'm good, thanks,' he replies. 'But how are you *feeling*? Are you feeling sad, anxious, worried, indifferent? It's important that you recognise your feelings,' she insists. Mr Pokerface plays along, 'Ah yeah, I guess indifferent. I mean, I didn't know her very well.' Surely that's enough for this woman, he hopes. 'Yes, of course, but I mean she fell down the stairs and died ... today ... in this house. Surely that evokes some sort of a feeling inside of you?'

Mr Pokerface feels like he's back in the one therapy session he was made to sit through after he broke up with his most recent ex. 'Well, what are *you* feeling?' he asks Ms Boulder. He remembered, from that one session, the trick of feigning empathy. Although the therapist didn't call it 'feigning', she called it being interested in the other person. 'Well, I guess I'm feeling saddened by the news and a little shocked. I feel awkward that we're expected to enjoy a meal she cooked right before she died. Maybe we should go around the table and each share something nice about Ms Prettyeyes? It might help us connect to her,' suggests Ms Boulder.

Meanwhile, the dinner party is interrupted by a policeman who's talking to Jeeves in the lobby. The guests drop into silence so that they can eavesdrop on their conversation. 'We don't think this was an accident,' the policeman states. 'We believe Ms Prettyeyes was murdered and nobody is leaving this house until we have taken statements. Everyone is a suspect.' All of a sudden, a roar of thunder rolls through, causing the plates on the dining table to shake. A bolt of lightning strikes the tin roof of the garden shed and the power goes out in the manor, leaving the guests in a cloak of darkness. Everyone jumps and screams in unison, including Mr Pokerface who finally seems to be feeling something – shit scared.

Ms Fountain shrieks and then bursts back into tears. Mr Compassion holds her tight and starts sobbing too. Ms Brainy, for the first time that evening, is no longer in her head and instead feels fearful as her heart rate picks up and she struggles to breathe. Mr Pokerface got a bloody fright and feels adrenaline pulsating through his body. Ms Boulder repeats to herself, 'I am safe, I am safe, I am safe,' and encourages Mr Pokerface to repeat it alongside her. The first course hasn't even arrived yet but I'm going to stop the tale of this party right here.

Okay, so whodunnit?! No, this isn't a murder mystery party. Nobody is the bad guy here. Ms Prettyeyes did indeed just fall down the stairs. This story was never about her death or the dinner, it was about the guests. It's easy to see that when faced with the news of the death of their host, each guest's reaction varies. They are all aware that the death of someone is a sad event, yet the way in which they each process it is very different.

When, however, they're caught off guard by the loss of power after the delivery of the news of a murder taking place, their bodies don't have time to process it cerebrally and instead they just feel the immediate physical reactions and a flood of feelings. Of course, each guest is a dramatisation of certain emotional types and you may not relate to one of the guests in their entirety, but I believe we can adopt qualities from all of them. Let's have a look at the strengths and weaknesses of each guest.

The overly emotional Ms Fountain

Super sensitivity is an enviable trait to those who can feel nothing, but feeling everything can be a burden if you can't support yourself and process the emotions rather than marinate in them and become victim to your circumstance. It's unlikely that Ms Fountain had ever questioned why she was so emotional, if it was appropriate to be so emotional in a room full of strangers and if her emotional outburst was overshadowing everyone else's experience.

Strengths: Being able to feel your feelings as they arise can be a really good way to ensure feelings are being processed and not suppressed. It's likely they can easily recognise and validate other people's feelings.

Weaknesses: They can be overly dramatic and unsure of when to let the feeling go. It's possible that they can't decipher between different feelings. They can also be prone to becoming a victim.

What we can adopt from them: Allowing yourself to feel your feelings fully will allow them to move through you faster. And, of course, we can't dismiss the old adage: better out than in.

The insensitive bastard Mr Pokerface

You've likely dated this type, I know I certainly have. But let's kick off by saying bastard is a harsh descriptor (and definitely politically incorrect) and just because somebody can't identify their feelings, it doesn't mean they're not having any. Insensitivity is defined as a lack of concern for other people's feelings but what I've come to realise is that sometimes what we perceive as insensitivity is actually someone struggling to recognise an emotion, even if it's slapped them in the face.

Strengths: Stays calm in a crisis.

Weaknesses: Lacks not just the ability to articulate their feelings but also the ability to recognise them.

What we can adopt from them: Well, not a lot other than to work on recognising different feelings as they arise in the body.

The intellectual processor Ms Brainy

You don't have to be an A+ smartypants to be classified as this type but you're likely someone who spends a lot of time thinking (most likely overthinking) and trying to find logic in feelings. I'll put my hand up and say this is me to a tee. But not all feelings can be rationalised, which can make for a very frustrating experience (am I right, fellow overthinkers?). Also, you can't actually process an emotion through the mind. Labelling our emotions is wonderful, but then you have to *embody* the feeling, which means processing it through your body. Feeling it, even when it's uncomfortable AF. This has been my lifelong struggle. I have no issue identifying an emotion and working out why I'm feeling it but when it comes to feeling it and letting it wash through me, I get bored and either hold back the tears or just let them half pour out and then I move on.

Strengths: Logical and rational. They have no issue solving problems and can stay calm in emotional situations.

Weaknesses: They can appear as insensitive and give off the impression of being cold. They can have trouble connecting with feelings, are prone to over-analysis and can skip the embodying process, which means feelings just keep resurfacing.

What we can adopt from them: It's advantageous to ask yourself how you feel and label that feeling but then you have to feel it. Having the awareness of that feeling being processed and moving on is something that Ms Fountain and the rest of us could adopt from Ms Brainy.

The empathic hero Mr Compassion

Empaths take on other people's feelings as if they were their own, which becomes emotionally exhausting for the empath and confusing because it's tricky to decipher what emotions are theirs and what emotions belong to someone else. The biggest issue I've witnessed with empaths (and I am one myself) is that it's often worn as both a burden and a badge of honour. It does make you compassionate and caring but not if it's at the expense of your own emotions and energy. In order to feel helpful or useful at that party, Mr Compassion had to be supporting someone else's emotions.

Strengths: Fantastic helper and friend. They're very supportive and intuitive. They're able to recognise feelings in themselves and others with ease.

Weaknesses: The lines often get blurred over what emotions are theirs and what emotions belong to others. They can have issues setting boundaries and easily absorb other people's negativity.

What we can adopt from them: Without empathy, we can end up a lot like the insensitive bastard Mr Pokerface. Empathy is an important tool for connecting with others and supporting their emotions. Empaths make great listeners and when in a crisis, they're a good ally. We chat more about empathy later in this chapter.

The stable Ms Boulder

Ms Boulder looks like the shining example of emotional stability. You'll notice that she's great at supporting others and initiating calming techniques but when the question of, 'How are *you* feeling?' is posed to her, she struggles to respond. Ms Boulder is similar to Mr Compassion in that she is there to offer support but differs in that she doesn't absorb the emotions of everyone else.

Strengths: They're dependable and stable. They don't react to other people's emotions or place judgement.

Weaknesses: They find it easier to listen than to share their own feelings. They're unlikely to initiate conversations about their own feelings and prefer to play the role of therapist.

What we can adopt from them: Their ability to stay cool in a crisis and check in on their peers is nothing to be scoffed at. But if they can learn to take their own advice and ask themselves how they're feeling every now and then, they would benefit greatly.

There's actually a sixth emotional type that I've encountered so many times in my life that I couldn't go on without introducing them. They weren't at the party but they're definitely worth a mention.

The cool, calm and collected (but freaking out on the inside)

You might know this emotional type as the overly emotional person wearing the cloak of the insensitive bastard. This is a recipe for disaster. Let's look at it with a visual cue … Outside is a wall of impenetrable steel; inside is an overflowing fountain. The water from the fountain (or in this case, emotions) has nowhere to go. The impenetrable steel has built a facade of, 'Oh, I'm so fine. I've absolutely got my shit together,' but those emotions aren't actually being expressed so they continue overflowing with nowhere to go and, eventually, one of two things will happen: they'll either explode (likely at an inopportune time) or manifest somewhere else. The especially tricky thing about this emotional type is that people treat them like the insensitive bastard but in actual fact they're not!

Exercise 8

WHICH DINNER GUEST ARE YOU?

We each have our own emotional 'filter'. It affects the way we perceive and present to the world and it's the reason why people's reactions to the same situations can vary (like with Ms Prettyeyes's dinner party guests). Get curious about which of the six different emotional types from the adorable dinner party tale you identify with. Remember, you could be a combination of a few.

1. The overly emotional Ms Fountain

2. The insensitive bastard Mr Pokerface

3. The intellectual processor Ms Brainy

4. The empathic hero Mr Compassion

5. The stable Ms Boulder

6. The cool, calm and collected (but freaking out on the inside)

At this point, we're just trying to get to know ourselves better. Perhaps you were also able to recognise the emotional tendencies of the people around you. When I realised that the way I process and express emotion is different to my peers, I found that I had more compassion for them and myself. BONUS!

PROCESSING YOUR EMOTIONS

We're going to jump right into an exercise before I tell you anything about processing emotions. It's a rather backwards way of teaching but this is a book about self-awareness and I think it's important that you're aware of who you are now before I start encouraging you to look at things from new perspectives or to try techniques you've never tried before. Make sense?

Exercise 9
EMOTIONAL PROCESSING

Ask yourself: how do I process emotions? By this, I mean when you feel something, how do you deal with the emotions that come up? Instead of writing down what you think is the right way to process emotions, I want you to write down what you actually do (FYI, there's no 'right' way, everyone just processes emotions differently).

Here are some examples to prompt you:

(A wave of feeling comes your way and you switch off and distract yourself with a phone call, a show on Netflix or a glass of wine.

(You become overwhelmed by emotion and feel like you can't manage or understand exactly what you're feeling.

(You rationalise the feeling by trying to find logic and reason around why you feel the way you feel.

(You allow yourself space to feel the emotion and you find that it eventually passes.

(You find it easy to feel certain emotions over others. Perhaps anger and guilt come easily to you but you numb out on sadness and grief.

(You have volcanic emotions, meaning you act on all emotions despite destructive consequences.

(Emotions ... what are they?

Just as there were different emotional types and you could be a combination of a few, the same goes for the way you process emotions. But in general, what is your standard way to deal with emotions as they arise?

We've been socially conditioned to avoid feeling and expressing emotions, with women labelled as unstable and men labelled as weak. So if you found that your emotional process was to suppress, ignore or distract yourself from your emotions, you are not alone. This is normal! But just because society is behind the times when it comes to being in touch with feelings, that doesn't mean you can't learn to process your feelings more effectively.

Have you ever heard a therapist or self-help author tell you to just 'feel your feelings'? I believe it was an instruction I offered in *Make It Happen*, but there was good reason behind this prompt. You see, when we actually *feel* our feelings, rather than think them or bypass them altogether, we can change our vibrational frequency and see the real impact that our feelings have on our manifestation practice. But how does one actually feel their feelings? And why is it so bloody important? I'm going to start with the latter. It's important to note that unfelt feelings aren't just feelings that are ignored or suppressed but also feelings that are misunderstood, unmanaged, marinated in or not processed at all. Here's an analogy that illustrates why we can't just ignore our feelings.

You know when you mute someone on Instagram and then all of a sudden it's as if they don't exist? You don't see them posting photos that make you feel unworthy, they're no longer selling you their new product and their seemingly perfect life just disappears. Then, in passing one day, a friend mentions them and you're like, 'Oh yeah, what happened to them? They just fell off the radar, hey?', to which your friend replies, 'What? No, they're still as big as ever. You just stopped following them.' Well, this is what happens to your feelings when you mute them. They don't go away even if you temporarily forget they exist. They're still there building their profile, selling teeth-whitening products (not really, but you get my point) and living their 'best life'.

Note: don't mute your feelings, but I give you full permission to mute people on Instagram that make you feel shitty.

Here's another great analogy I stumbled across to illustrate why you have to pay attention to your feelings. When you're busy numbing out, ignoring or suppressing your feelings, your feelings don't just disappear – they're in the other room doing ab-curls and push-ups. Then, when you're done with your bottle of wine, Netflix binge session or any other unhelpful distraction you've concocted to avoid them, you'll walk into the other room and realise that your feelings are bigger than before because you gave them all that time to work out and now they're ready to rumble! So, before we all start an army of pumped-up, gym-fiend emotions, let's have a look at what it really means to 'feel your feelings' and process your emotions.

Be aware of your avoidance go-tos

If you're going to learn to effectively process your emotions, it's helpful to recognise what tools you currently use to avoid feeling them. Here are some common avoidance techniques:

★ Alcohol, drugs and food (think more ice cream and doughnuts than broccoli and kale).
★ Busyness. This is my go-to avoidance trick. 'Yeah, I'm waaaay too busy to have time to feel sad today.'
★ Video games, TV, social media = self-explanatory.
★ Investing too heavily in other people's problems in an attempt to avoid dealing with your own. You might also find you're an incredible advice giver when it comes to

other people's feelings but you refuse to do the same for yourself.

I'm not about to tell you to abandon all of these things, because everything mentioned above is fine in moderation, but only you can determine if they're being used in a way that allows you to avoid how you're really feeling.

Notice and name your feelings

I don't mean calling fear Fred and anxiety Arnold, but rather seeking to identify what feelings are arising for you and label them for what they are. It might sound straightforward, but you can't begin to process an emotion without first recognising that you're having it. This is about getting curious (which you're becoming well versed in), because emotions are tricky tricksters and aren't always how they first present.

Here are some things to consider:

★ Look for physical indicators. This could be a tightening in the chest, a lump in the throat, sweaty hands, a rapid heart rate or a sinking feeling in your gut. (In retrospect, I can see how some of these may also present as signs of a heart attack but I feel like you're in tune enough to recognise the difference.)

★ See if you're able to pinpoint what the emotion is and know that it might not be what first presents. This is where it's helpful to get curious. For example, is it anger that you're feeling or are you actually scared or confused and this has presented as anger? Perhaps you're feeling several emotions. That's fine too – they're all valid – just make sure you identify and label them all.

★ If you struggle with the words to pin to your emotions, I suggest looking online for a wheel of emotions chart. This can be so incredibly helpful to identify what you're feeling and show you what emotions are similar to each other.

★ Write down your emotions or speak them out loud (I do both). I like to write them down because I find them easier to unpack when I can see them. Other times, I find it can help to talk out feelings with a trusted confidant.

Did you know that naming and labelling what you're feeling actually helps your brain to process what you're experiencing? This is why talk therapy is so healing, even when it feels like you're not really learning anything new about yourself. Simply by expressing what you're feeling, you diminish the response of the amygdala (the brain's anxiety response centre). In other words, naming your emotions may help you to regulate them. The technical term is called 'affect labelling' and it basically means putting your feelings into words.

Quit judging

I waste so much time judging everything I feel and it mostly comes down to me comparing my circumstances to somebody else's. When I felt disappointed, devastated and confused about the state of the world during the pandemic, I told myself I was incredibly lucky and should feel grateful that I am safe, healthy and free. When I get sad that I haven't seen my family for a few months, I remind myself that there are people in my life that have lost family members to illness or old age. Someone will always be worse off than you but that doesn't make your feelings any less valid. Practise self-compassion and know that feelings don't require a jury to determine their validity or a reason for why they are surfacing in order for them to be true for you. Judging may also look like explaining a feeling away or defining what a feeling says about you as a person.

Feelings are not facts

Another important thing to remember is that feelings are not facts. I made this abundantly clear when I recounted my incessant sobbing over the (not actual) death of the fictional character Meredith Grey. Emotions can also surface over things that feel seemingly true but, on further investigation, are not. For example, you might feel devastated that a friend no longer enjoys your company because you haven't heard from them in a couple of weeks. You convince yourself the friendship is over and you feel emotions of anger, sadness, loss and guilt. Then, you get a phone call from them and learn they've had things going on in their life that have nothing to do with you. Does that mean that none of those things you felt were real? No, but it does mean that they weren't factual and it's important to be conscious of that when you're processing emotions. Before I get carried away with a feeling, I ask myself if there's any evidence to indicate this feeling is true, and if it could be helpful for me to learn more before making assumptions.

'Fred (aka fear), what are you trying to tell me?'

Emotions have a purpose. They're not just there to make you feel good or bad. They're indicators that help you to figure out how to deal with a particular situation or circumstance. Once you've noticed and named what you're feeling, it's helpful to get curious about why the feeling has surfaced. For example, if you're feeling lonely, has this feeling come to the surface to remind you that you need to organise some social engagements? Are you feeling lonely because you choose not to attend events you're invited to? Is this feeling of loneliness an indicator that it's time to make some changes in your life? Or sometimes we feel a feeling just because – that's okay too. Showing yourself compassion and saying 'I feel lonely today because I am alone' – full stop – is also helpful. You could then ask yourself what would make you feel less lonely today. My point is that, once again, curiosity is your best friend when it comes to effectively processing an emotion. Simply enquiring about what a feeling is trying to tell you can be so incredibly illuminating.

Accepting your emotions

We're about to move on to expressing your emotions but, just like the three steps of self-awareness, there is a step in between curiosity, which the above points were all trying to teach you: acceptance. In the context of processing emotions, we must lose any resistance against the feeling and, regardless of whether it's viewed as a positive or negative feeling, we need to accept it for what it is. What we often do instead of accept is abandon the experience in favour of something distracting, which takes us all the way back to our avoidance go-tos! Most of us are able to willingly accept positive emotions such as happiness, excitement and validation. Piece of cake! The war we wage tends to be activated when we're faced with less favourable emotions such as heartache, shame and despair. We also tend to avoid feelings and traits that we judge others for, such as desperation or laziness. But when we can practise acceptance, we're opening ourselves up to experiencing a whole spectrum of emotions and exploring them with equal validity and curiosity. As we've already learned throughout this book, the Law of Polarity teaches us that two extremes together make a whole. All feelings, negative and positive, need to be accepted in order for you to effectively process them and increase your emotional intelligence. Make sense?

Notice when you're sitting with an emotion longer than you need to

You may feel like the emotion has been processed, but if you use it to define you and make it a story that you consistently share with everyone, then you allow that emotion to dominate who you are. When you stay in an emotion longer than you need to and don't take responsibility for it, then you run the risk of slipping into victim mode.

Taking action and responsibility

When you notice a pattern with your emotions, such as anxiety always arising when you are in social situations or self-doubt emerging whenever you need to do a presentation at work, then it might be helpful to figure out what practices or systems you can introduce in order to effectively manage your emotions. In the two examples I just gave, a mindfulness practice would be beneficial. For you, it could be booking in some talk therapy or it may be as simple as giving yourself time and space to centre yourself and find your breath before putting yourself in those situations. Whatever the situation is, it's your responsibility to notice patterns within your emotional processing and take responsibility and conscious action to try something different. This is also very helpful if you've found yourself slipping into victim mode.

EXPRESS YOURSELF!

It's one thing to process your emotions, but you've also got to give them an escape route; otherwise they'll just fester inside of you. This is where healthy emotional expression comes into play. Before we get started learning new and healthy ways to express emotion, let's do a similar exercise to what we did with processing emotions and work out how you currently express yourself.

Exercise 10
EMOTIONAL EXPRESSION

Ask yourself: how do I currently express my emotions? Don't write what you think is the right way to express emotions. I want you to write down what you actually do because, once again, there's no 'right' way. Everyone expresses their emotions differently.

Here are some examples to prompt you:

⟨ Can I comfortably talk about and articulate my feelings?

⟨ Do I find it difficult to talk about how I'm feeling?

⟨ Do I find it difficult to contain emotions? For example, if
you're sad, do you find it difficult to stop crying even after
allowing yourself time to process the sadness?

⟨ Alternatively, do I find it difficult to access emotions? For
example, if you're feeling angry, can you label it as anger
but find it difficult to allow yourself to feel angry?

⟨ If I'm feeling something, is it evident in my body language
and facial expressions?

⟨ Do I find it easy to journal about my feelings?

⟨ Do I not allow adequate time to express emotions, which
causes them to build up and then explode out of me at
inopportune moments?

The practice of expressing emotions is a personal one that will differ from person to person. What's vital is that you find ways to express emotions that work for you, and this doesn't always mean a verbal and physical expression of that feeling in the moment. Not only will expressing emotions feel cathartic after processing the emotion (which we just ran through), but there are several studies that show healthy emotional expression comes with an array of positive health benefits, as well as studies that show suppressing negative emotions can lead to increased stress.

Here are some healthy ways to express an emotion:

★ Talk about it with a trusted friend. Ideally someone who will listen rather than someone who has an opinion about how you should be feeling.

★ Allow the body's physical manifestation of the feeling to come through. If you're sad, allow yourself space to cry. My tendency with crying is that I start off okay, but then within seconds I attempt to pull myself together and stop the expression too early. I'm not encouraging you to cry for days on end but allowing the tears to pour out of you until it feels like the right time to stop will likely allow the sadness to move through you more efficiently.

★ Moving the body is a great way to express emotions. Dancing to a good tune is my go-to way to move anger or anxiety through my body. It's not a distraction, but rather brings physicality to whatever thoughts are racing through my mind. You might prefer to go for a run or a swim instead.

★ Journal about how you're feeling. If you're not able to talk about your feelings, writing about them can be just as therapeutic.

★ Get creative! Perhaps you have an artistic flair and painting or drawing about how you feel works for you.

Whichever way you choose to express an emotion, know that it's always better out than in. When you finally quit suppressing an emotion, you will undoubtedly feel immense relief. You see, when we don't find a healthy expression for an emotion, not only does it fester inside of us and become an unknown timebomb waiting to explode, but we can also misdirect our feelings towards other people, which is a whole other disaster within itself.

MANIFESTATION REMINDER

Your emotions contribute to your energy, influence your vibrational frequency and affect your ability to manifest. So, nurture your emotional self by processing your emotions effectively and expressing them in a way that feels cathartic and releases them.

A quick word on dumping emotions ...

I always encourage emotions to be shared, as this can be helpful, but do you dump your emotions onto other people almost as if passing the baton? It's important to know that even if we share our feelings with others we're still the carriers of them. A feeling shared isn't a feeling dumped. Here's how emotional dumping can manifest:

★ You repeat the same conversation about how you're feeling over and over again.

- ★ You don't listen to or follow any advice or help that has been offered to you as a solution.
- ★ You're closed off to a mutual emotional exchange, such as listening to someone else's emotional expression.

When sharing your emotions with others, it's important to be aware of boundaries and to not allow your venting to become a violation of somebody else's emotional or energetic field. Plus, when we dump our emotions, we're bypassing the processing of them.

What if a feeling keeps resurfacing?

If a feeling keeps rearing its ugly head, it's a tell-tale sign of one of the following issues:

- ★ Something deeper hasn't been acknowledged.
- ★ An emotion running deeper is the cause of this current feeling.
- ★ You're playing out a pattern that you need to take responsibility for.

Self-awareness asks you to get curious, which is what you need to do in these situations. Keep asking yourself questions until you get to the root of what's making you feel an emotion. If you can't come to your own conclusion, it might be worth talking it out with a therapist or trusted friend. But be gentle with yourself. It's okay to hit snooze on a feeling when you can't deal with it in the moment. The important thing is that you do come back to it. Also, be conscious that some feelings are bigger and more layered than others, such as grief.

The deep abyss

Trigger warning about miscarriage

I sit here not just alone, but lonely. The phone calls and texts have stopped. People aren't sure what to say that they haven't already said, but I don't need to talk about it. I just want company, or am I looking for a distraction? My thoughts don't stop. I can't make sense of any of this. Why did this happen and what the fuck am I meant to do now? Carry on as if nothing has happened? As if my whole world hasn't just crumbled into a million pieces? Everyone's lives keep moving forward, but I'm stuck in a deep abyss of grief, not sure which way is out.

I count myself lucky to have got through three-and-a-half decades of my life without experiencing grief. I mean, I'd experienced emotionally tumultuous things before, such as the breakdown of relationships, death of grandparents and loss of family pets, but once real grief kisses you for the first time, you realise that nothing you've experienced before compares.

I contemplated sharing my experience of grief without divulging the specifics of my circumstance, but I believe it's the concealment of people's grief that makes it such an isolating experience. Society isn't conditioned to deal with it, which makes grief feel so unfamiliar – like you're the only one to ever experience such immense pain in the history of existence. My hope is that by sharing my story with you, you're able to connect with it in a way that serves either your own experience of loss or enables you to understand someone else's experience of loss. Because that's what grief is: a natural response to loss. I used to think grief was just another word for sad, but it is so much more than feeling sad. Grief is specific to the loss of someone or something – usually from death – and is a mixed bag of feelings including, but not limited to, sadness, anger, fatigue, anxiety, fear, disbelief and guilt.

My grief arrived in the form of a miscarriage at 12 weeks. It's not a long period in the scheme of your entire life, but long enough to bond with a baby you'll never meet. I have friends who'd experienced miscarriages before me and each time I empathised with their loss, but until you've physically felt that pain, you just don't know what it truly feels like. The pain is so visceral. Emotionally, of course, but then there's the physical pain – the intense contractions, the massive blood loss, the excruciating heartache. No one speaks of the toll it takes on your physical body. It's an imitation of labour without the reward. The grief of any loss swallows you whole, but when your physical body has literal skin in the game, it adds an extra layer of devastation that I still haven't been able to muster the words for. In the days following my miscarriage, there were fleeting moments where I'd forget that a baby isn't something that you can just get back after you've lost it. When you break up with a partner, there is always the possibility that you could make amends, but a miscarriage – like any other death – is final. When they're gone, they're gone and this was something I struggled to intellectualise for quite some time.

I don't think it's fair to compare one miscarriage to another. However, in the grieving process of my experience, it was incredibly complicated because I was grieving so much more than just the loss of a baby. My pregnancy was an unexpected but treasured surprise. I'd experienced a very uncharacteristic summer fling and two weeks after our relationship ended, I found myself sitting on the couch with a girlfriend taking an at-home pregnancy test. 'It won't be positive,' I insisted. 'I'm 36. I think I'd know if I was pregnant. I'm just late.' It turns out I wouldn't know if I was pregnant because there were two very clear lines on that test and I was indeed with child. I'd always thought that the moment I found out I was pregnant would be a time of utter elation. My husband and I would be over the moon, keeping the little secret between ourselves until we decided to share the news collectively with our loved ones. But here I was – single, pregnant and drowning in a tsunami of mixed emotions and indecision. 'It's positive,' my girlfriend reiterated, as if I hadn't registered exactly what those two lines meant. 'I can't be pregnant. No! This isn't how it was meant to happen. I can't have this baby. Absolutely not.' I remember those words so clearly now. If I hadn't said them so fervently, would I still be growing that baby inside of me? If I'd fully appreciated it as a gift in those first few moments rather than a very big problem, would the universe have punished me so brutally?

After three tumultuous days of indecision, many tears, a few heated debates and a little bit of excitement, I made the life-altering decision to become a single mother. That moment changed everything. I fell so deeply in love with the tiny human growing inside of me. I won't go into the painful details of the miscarriage but, when it happened (over three agonising days), I lost so much more than a baby. I lost my future. I lost the sense of relief I'd experienced so fleetingly when I thought that I wasn't going to be a childless woman any longer. I'd also convinced myself that I lost my last opportunity to have a baby. When I made the decision to go ahead with the pregnancy at age 36, I had to realistically consider that this might be my only hope. 'Just try again,' one of the nurses in the ER reassured me. But when you don't have a partner, there isn't an opportunity to just try again, which for me made the grief, loss and inconsolable madness that kept me awake at night so torturous, overwhelming and downright crippling. Was it a fact? No, of course there will be other opportunities for me to have a baby, but there was so much unknown and I didn't have the privilege of just trying again next month. Three of my closest friends were also pregnant, which was one of the most excruciating parts of the process. Not only did I lose my baby, but I also, for a period of time, lost my friends. I couldn't be around them, as I couldn't handle their happy baby news, pregnancy milestones or baby showers. To make it worse, my miscarriage became a burden to them, as they experienced guilt for continuing to have healthy pregnancies when I couldn't.

I don't recount any of this for sympathy, but rather for connection. When we grieve a loss, it's rarely just the one thing we lose. For me, it was a baby, a future, my friends, my hope, my sparkle (it took me five long months to get even half of my sparkle back) and, if I'm being honest, I also lost my faith. For others, it could be their job, their independence, their financial security and their safety net. We can't rush grief, as it's incredibly layered, profoundly deep and fucking complicated. There is no rule book. Everyone will experience loss to different degrees, in different ways, with differing variables and circumstances. But what I do know about grief is that it moves in waves. Grief is non-linear. It doesn't have a timeframe or an end date. There will be days when you remember what it's like to laugh and feel positive, and swiftly you'll be met with guilt and shame for allowing a smile to cross your face. Just because you can belly laugh one day, it doesn't mean you've forgotten or you've healed. This was something I struggled with for a long time after my loss, as I started to recognise parts of myself again that had vanished when in the thick of it all, and I felt hope start to creep back in. If you can relate to this, know that nobody is judging your happiness. In fact, they're celebrating it. Nobody expects you to pick up the pieces as if nothing is broken. Your grief is yours and you're free to experience it in whatever way feels good to you.

It's been five months since my miscarriage and, I tell you, there's no way I could have contemplated writing this even a month ago without completely breaking. My grief hurt so much that most days I struggled to breathe, but over time the rhythmic effortlessness of breathing returned. So, if you're reading this still in the thick of your own grief and it feels as if the grief may never go away, I promise you one day it won't hurt this much. I once read a great quote on Instagram that said, 'People tend to think grief shrinks over time, but what really happens is that we grow around our grief,' and I wholeheartedly believe this to be true.

Grief is complex and when it comes to emotionally processing and expressing it, the tips I gave you earlier may be difficult to apply – that's okay too. Grief requires patience, compassion and surrender. I'd like to share with you a few things that helped me, if not to help you deal with your own grief, then maybe to help someone else deal with theirs.

In the early days of grief:

* Find people who you're comfortable talking to about the grief. The role of these people is to listen. It's hard to process advice when the pain is so raw, but it's helpful to be able to speak about how you're feeling.

* Don't try to use reason and logic to explain why the loss has occurred. The notion that 'everything happens for a reason' is not helpful in moments of grief and if you want to abandon your spirituality temporarily and have stern words with the universe or God, then that's absolutely fine. In fact, I found this therapeutic.

* If you're supporting someone who is grieving, remember to check in on them even after time has passed. I found that texts and phone calls dried up after the two-week mark, and that was when I really started to feel everything because the shock had started to wear off.

* Outsource life for a while. Get a house cleaner, organise some home-cooked meals, get friends and family to pick up the kids from school. Loved ones want to be able to help you, so if friends ask what you need or what they can do to help, ask them to cook you some food, watch the kids or do the laundry. This will make them feel helpful and it will keep you nourished.

* I found myself becoming a bit of a recluse, as I was too scared to face the world in case something triggered me in public. However, when my friends did manage to drag me outside for a beach walk or an ocean swim, I found

that the things I built up in my head weren't nearly as daunting as I'd imagined.

★ You can't cry too much in the early days of grief. Crying is therapeutic and cleansing, and if you allow the tears to flow often, I promise you one day they will stop or at least be less frequent.

★ Avoid numbing techniques like alcohol and drugs but allow yourself to get lost in re-runs of your favourite TV shows or anything that elicits a giggle. My saviours were *Ted Lasso* and *Will & Grace* re-runs.

★ Search for things that put you in a state of awe. I listened to the audio version of Julia Baird's book *Phosphorescence* when I was in deep healing. She speaks about how it's difficult to strive for happiness or joy when you're experiencing darkness in the form of grief or depression, but you can seek things that put you in a state of awe. For me, this was whale watching from the Byron Bay lighthouse and catching the sunrise and sunset each day. Seeking awe became a very healing practice in my recovery.

In the next stages of grief:

★ I found talk therapy really helpful. I'm blessed to have friends who I can talk with freely, but there was something healing about talking to a therapist who wasn't emotionally invested in my story. I also found that we were able to break the overwhelming blanket of grief into smaller pieces of a patchwork quilt and process them one patch at a time. Once I got to this stage, I found I was able to process and express emotions with a lot more ease.

★ I'm a huge advocate for energy work and I tried a lot of things during the grieving process. Kinesiology, acupuncture, reiki and homeopathy all helped to some degree, but the most transformational therapy I received was an energy technique called Havening. Now, I've tried a butt-load of alternative therapies in my time and they all have their own benefits, but after just one Havening session, I significantly reduced the trauma around my miscarriage. I was able to start leaving the house of my own accord, seeing my pregnant friends again and visiting friends with newborns. My appetite came back and I stopped crying at the drop of a hat. If you've never heard of Havening before, it seems a little bit woo woo but it's based on neuroscience. Plus, Justin Bieber is a fan, so SOLD! Havening is a technique that uses sensory input like touch to change how the brain functions. During a typical Havening session, a patient will recall a traumatic memory and a trained therapist will use gentle touch on their hands, arms or face (I did my session via Zoom and did the touching myself), while different distraction techniques are introduced by the therapist. The idea is that because your brain is unable to process two thoughts at the same time, the soft touch removes the trauma memory and halts activation of the amygdala – the part of the brain responsible for processing emotions. The distractions include counting to 20, saying the alphabet, spelling your name, reciting your phone number, basically anything that serves as a distraction. Of all the alternative therapies I've tried in my lifetime, this was the most immediate, effective and permanent. You're welcome.

★ Put yourself in situations you think you won't be able to handle. I know this sounds harsh, but you're so much more resilient than you think you are and if you spend your time using your grief as an excuse, you'll never be able to live life to its fullest. This is where the real healing happens.

EMPATHY

The last subject in this chapter on emotions explores how you handle other people's emotions. It's an important component of increasing your emotional intelligence and I truly believe that once you have a grasp on your own emotional process, you'll be able to understand other people's emotional processes with more ease. The ability to feel what another person is feeling from their perspective is what we know as empathy, but let's first have a look at how you respond to other people's emotions.

Exercise 11

EMPATHY FOR THE DEVIL

Okay, so it was 'Sympathy For The Devil' and The Rolling Stones hold zero relevance here, but if you can take a minute to empathise with the difficulty of coming up with punchy headlines all the time, you might be able to let this one slide. Speaking of ... let's get curious about how you engage with other people's emotions.

Ask yourself:

❰ Am I sensitive to other people's emotions?

❰ Would I classify myself as an empath?

❰ Am I able to separate my emotions from other people's emotions?

Again, there are no right or wrong answers here, just things for you to contemplate.

I've always considered myself a very empathetic gal (FYI, most people are), but strong self-awareness allows you to know when you're too heavily invested in other people's emotions, which I have been far too often in the past. It's likely you have too. Perhaps a friend is going through a heavy break-up and instead of just being there for her and providing comfort and compassion, you also start feeling her despair, heartache and anger as if it's your own. Many of us wear the label of empath as a badge of honour, and although it's admirable to a degree, it's not a redeeming quality when it's at the expense of your own emotions and energy. Ya feel me?

It's normal to be sensitive to other people's feelings – in fact, it's an exemplary quality, especially when you're very close to that person – and it's essential when forming intimate relationships, but it's vital to be able to empathise from a healthy space. Where sympathy is the act of feeling *for* someone (for example, 'I'm so sorry you're sad'), empathy involves feeling *with* someone (for example, 'I feel your sadness'). It involves two people: the person we are feeling for and ourselves. Healthy empathy is learning to be able to put yourself in someone else's shoes while still keeping a clear distinction between what is theirs and what is yours, otherwise empathy can become a slippery slope into your own emotional depletion, and ain't nobody got time for that. The art of empathy requires:

★ Paying attention to another's needs without sacrificing your own.
★ The ability to distinguish between your feelings and their feelings.
★ The ability to look at things from someone else's perspective, even when you don't agree.
★ The ability to recognise emotions in others.
★ An acceptance of boundaries – both yours and theirs.

If you find that you do fall into being overly empathic, all that's required is a little self-awareness (which you're totally kicking ass at, by the way). When empathy is aroused within you, it's time to get curious and ask yourself these questions:

★ What am I feeling right now?
★ Are these my feelings or theirs?
★ What do I require at this moment?

Once you can determine what you need, you can make a conscious decision about how much of yourself you're willing to give to another at the expense of yourself. Once you start noticing the ways in which you become too absorbed in other people's emotions, especially their negative ones, you can create healthy boundaries or, in some cases, distance. We're going to talk about boundaries in more depth in Chapter 5.

I found it really helpful when I discovered that many psychologists break down empathy into three different types:

1. **Cognitive empathy:** This is the intellectual version of empathising. It's empathising by thought rather than by feeling and allowing yourself to see something from someone else's perspective. This is a very effective type of empathy in the workplace, as it allows you to put yourself in someone else's shoes without necessarily engaging with them emotionally.

2. **Emotional empathy:** Have you ever felt like you 'caught' someone's emotions like you would a common cold? Emotional empathy is when you literally feel the emotions of the other person alongside them. This is a highly covetable skill when managed correctly because it enables us to relate to how someone else is feeling. But, as indicated earlier, when we become consumed by someone else's emotions, it can be to our own detriment.

3. **Compassionate empathy:** I'd say that in most instances, this is the most appropriate form of empathy. People don't

need you to just understand them (cognitive empathy) or to feel and possibly crumble under the weight of their emotions (emotional empathy), they want you to understand and sympathise with what they're going through and help them to take action to resolve the problem, which is compassionate empathy. In choosing compassionate empathy, you're finding a good balance between logic and emotion while respecting your own boundaries and emotional capacity.

In summary: be empathetic, absolutely – it's a foundational part of human connection – but ensure that it's infused with self-awareness, compassion, personal boundaries and self-preservation.

MANIFESTATION REMINDER

You want your personal vibration to be 100 per cent authentic to you and taking on other people's 'stuff' is going to impact that. Be aware of how you absorb, manage and engage with other people's emotions, and get clear about what's yours and what's theirs. Make sense?

EMOTIONS AND THE THREE STEPS OF SELF-AWARENESS

Holy moly, you've learned a lot about your emotional self in this chapter! Now it's time to use the three steps of self-awareness to ensure you're using all of this new-found knowledge to become more self-aware, rather than be that annoying guest at dinner parties who sounds emotionally intelligent just because they read Goleman's book.

Step 1: Curiosity

In this chapter, you did several exercises to get curious about your emotional self. If you skipped past the exercises, it's imperative that you go back and do them. If emotions are a tricky subject for you and you really struggle with understanding and accessing them, please know that it just takes practice and patience (and this really helpful book you're reading). If you're looking for some extracurricular lines of enquiry around your emotional self, you might like to contemplate the following:

★ Are you able to process and express your emotions in certain environments, but not in others? If so, why? (For example, at work and in social situations your EQ is high, but in relationships you turn into an emotional mess.)

★ Are your emotions exacerbated by certain people? If so, is it because they're emotionally dumping on you? Or are they unable to support your emotional needs?

Step 2: Acceptance

When I walked you through some hot tips for processing your emotions with more ease, you discovered that a vital step is accepting your emotions. I think it's worth reiterating that point here. Only once you can accept feelings as they arise – and in a wider sense, your emotional type and tendencies – and let go of any resistance, especially to those icky feelings we try to avoid, can you begin to allow emotions to successfully move through you. When you don't, and only allow yourself to feel positive emotions such as happiness, joy and excitement, you're messing with the Law of Polarity. If you want to truly experience high-vibe emotions to their fullest, you must learn to feel the polar-opposite emotions too. Trust me, the sooner you start to process the challenging ones, the sooner they're released to make way for not only feel-good emotions to flood in, but also your manifestations. Woo hoo!

Step 3: Embodiment

Someone who's able to truly embody what it means to process, manage and express their emotions effectively is likely to have the following traits:

- ★ They're in tune with their own feelings.
- ★ They're able to articulate how they're feeling and what they require emotionally.
- ★ They're in tune with how others are feeling.
- ★ They're able to empathise without compromising on their own emotional self.
- ★ They're able to regulate their emotions.
- ★ They're willing and able to discuss feelings with others.
- ★ They're great listeners.
- ★ They're curious and can find the underlying cause of their emotion.
- ★ They're responsive, rather than reactive.

It's taken me a long time to truly understand my emotional self and I still learn new things every day. Improving your emotional intelligence isn't something that happens overnight. It's a constant evaluation of your own emotional processes, expression and responses, as well as the responses of those around you. So don't rush it; just know that if you can implement the three steps of self-awareness whenever big emotions arise, you're already so much closer to understanding who you are.

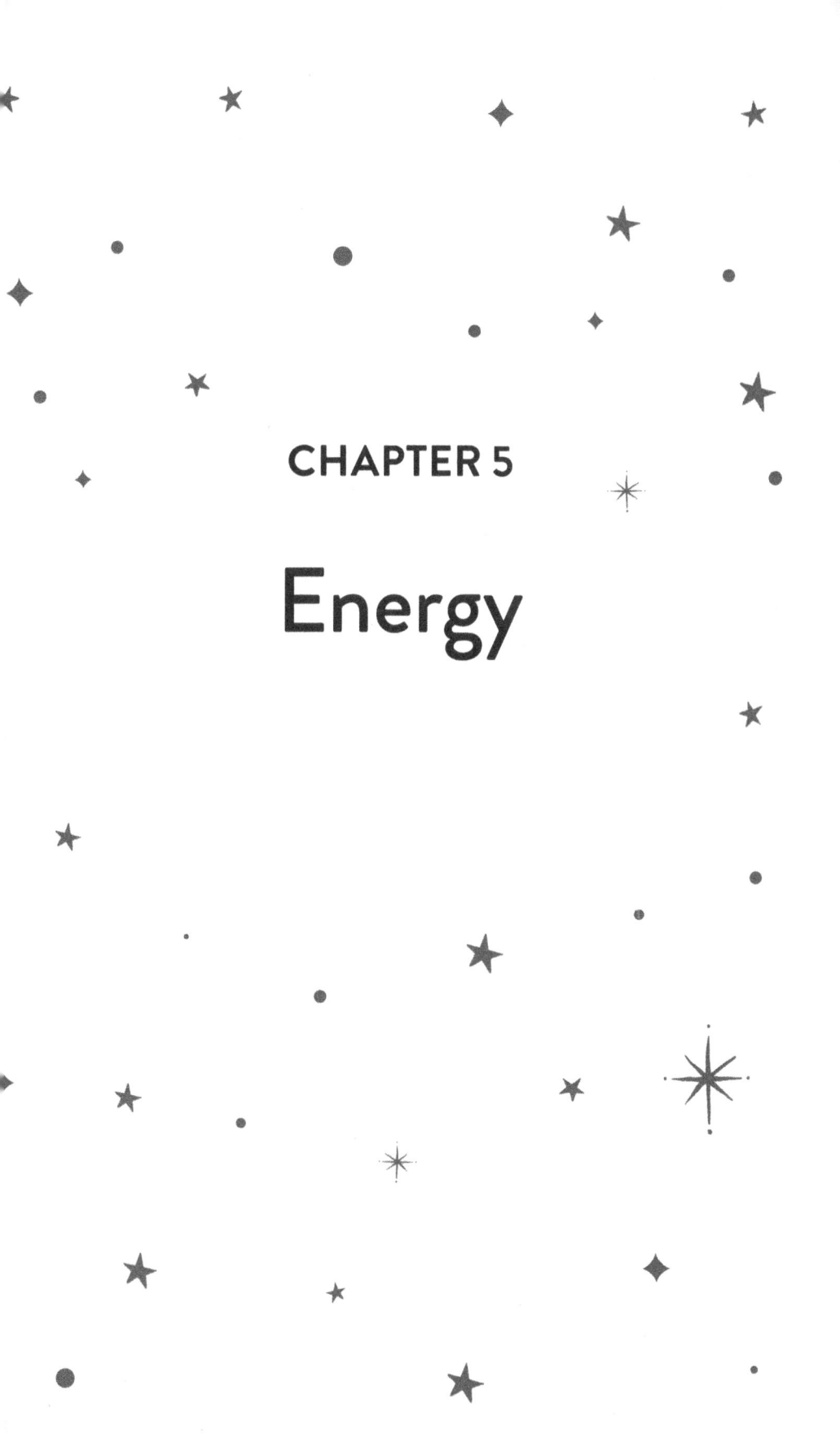

CHAPTER 5

Energy

I've never been someone who can survive on little sleep. I distinctly remember in my early 20s trying to keep up with my friends who could stay out until 3am and then arrive at work the next morning bright-eyed and bushy-tailed for a 6am start on the coffee machine. As I struggled to remember orders, pop the lids on the takeaway cups and give out the correct change, my colleagues (and party pals) were as fresh as bloody daisies – smiling, dazzling and joking with customers. Even when alcohol, hours of dancing in stilettos and minimal shut-eye was taken out of the mix, I still couldn't keep up with the energetic stamina of my friends. I'd walk into large social gatherings armed with my bubbly personality, gift for subtle flirting and sparkling conversation, and then moments later I'd want to extract myself faster than a fighter pilot evacuating a plummeting plane in order to go home and crawl into bed. Just as some athletes are made for endurance events, some for sharp sprints and others were just never made to be athletes at all, our energetic capacity to socialise, back it up after little sleep, exercise ourselves into perfection and work ridiculously long hours each day differs from person to person. Having an awareness and also acceptance (that's the clincher) of your own energetic capacity – as well as the most efficient way for you to recharge your own energy – will not only give you a whole new lease on life, but you'll find out that you've likely been missing out on boundless energy you didn't even know was at your disposal.

Society is set up for the type of person who can pull an eight–ten-hour day at work five times a week, get up early to exercise for an hour before said workday, socialise with friends and family after work and on the weekends, and be there to support and hold space for their loved ones. Then you throw kids into the mix, a sick parent that needs caring for, dogs that need to be walked and study that needs to be squeezed in, as well as time to clean the house, water the garden, service the car, take the bins out, cook and nourish yourself, take your supplements, meditate (my God, I hope you're making time to meditate) and then, if you're lucky, make room for a passion project on the side. It's energetically exhausting to read about it, let alone live it. It's been a massive struggle of mine for many, many years – even after I knew from evidence and experimentation that I wasn't wired energetically like other people – to accept that doing less actually enabled me to do more.

Honestly, I think it's a struggle for most people to honour their energetic needs. We all want to be the energiser bunny, usually because we all know one, and they set the standard for energy exertion. But once you can accept how YOUR energy works, you'll realise that there is a very small percentage of people who actually thrive at that pace. As we move through this chapter doing our curiosity cha-cha and learning new moves and steps along the way (how's this dancing analogy going?), I want you to be open-minded about what your energy responds to – even when it seems counterproductive – and I solemnly swear that you will notice profound improvements in your energy once you can listen to your body and respond accordingly.

INTROVERSION VERSUS EXTROVERSION

I'm an introvert. This doesn't make me shy, terrible at socialising or afraid of public speaking. In fact, I'm pretty bloody great at talking to strangers, making friends and addressing large groups from a public stage. It does mean, however, that I need adequate time on my own (often), I work best when I'm in solitude and silence and that being overstimulated by people, sounds, erratic winds and bright lights will deplete my energy faster than it would my extroverted friends. It's the reason I struggle at music festivals and concerts. Not because I don't love live music, but because I can't handle the combination of crowds of people, loud, layered sounds, strobe lights and no escape. As I've become more accepting of what it means to be introverted and how leaning into those tendencies not only makes me feel incredibly seen but also allows me to recharge my battery (which was very flat by the time I learned how to do introversion better), I've realised that I'd much rather be considered a party pooper than feel physically ill for staying out at a party longer than I wanted to out of obligation. It took me a long time to arrive at this point, mostly because life is conditioned for extroverts to thrive, but it's time for my fellow introverts to take centre stage (but only if you want to and feel comfortable. If you'd rather be alone inside and read, that's okay too). If you're an extrovert reading this (the next exercise will help you decide), then I guarantee you have some introverted friends who will benefit from you understanding them a little better.

In my 20s, I was so social. I had people around me all the fucking time and it was exhausting. I remember one day locking myself in my room, turning off my phone and drawing the blinds just so I could get a few hours to myself before a neighbour, friend or colleague came knocking on my front door (quite literally – I lived and worked in a Melrose Place of sorts and it was as fun as it was socially depleting). I was the same as a child. Friends would come over to play and when I'd had enough, I'd ask Mum to send them home so I could go into my room and read to decompress. It's not that introverts don't enjoy socialising – because we very much do – it's just that we feel physically, emotionally and energetically drained afterwards.

Looking at introverts and extroverts from an energetic standpoint allows you to understand each of them better, and hopefully (and most importantly) yourself. For so long, extroverts were viewed as the loud, gregarious performers and introverts were the shy, rude loners, but that's just not the case. There are a multitude of online tests that will help you decipher if you lean more towards introversion or extroversion (FYI, there's also a possibility that you're an ambivert, who is someone who has a balance of extrovert and introvert features). It's worth knowing because, once you do, you're able to direct your energy where it's most valued and energised, and not feel guilty when you need to pull back.

INTROVERT	EXTROVERT
Recharges their energy by being alone and in their own space.	Recharges their energy by being around other people and by engaging with their environment.
Values one-on-one interactions or small groups.	Values being in large groups.
Prefers working quietly and autonomously.	Prefers working in groups and open office settings.
Thinks before they speak.	Tends to think as they speak.
Reserved.	Outgoing.
Enjoys alone time and their independence.	Prefers the company of others and can be dependent on others.
Considered.	Risk takers.
Contemplative and reactive.	Active and jump right in.
Prefers to focus on one or two things at a time.	Prefers a variety of things so they don't get bored.
Easily overstimulated by sound, lights, stimulants and people.	Thrives off stimulation.

Exercise 13

ARE YOU AN INTROVERT OR AN EXTROVERT?

Factoring in the above table, do you feel you are more introverted or extroverted? Dispel any preconceived ideas and base it on how your energy is affected by the above. Like I said, I'm very social, enjoy attending parties and love public speaking, but only because I know how to manage my energy in between such engagements.

> If I didn't spend adequate time alone with minimal stimulation and work autonomously, I'd find it harder to embrace those moments on stage or be social with friends.

Often introverts will fake extroversion in order to fit in. Most of the time this is done subconsciously, but what pseudo-extroverts will find is that after spending their time trying to keep up with their extroverted counterparts, they'll get home and collapse in a heap (like me back in my 20s). While someone who is not self-aware might put this down to something as simple as fatigue or burning the candle at both ends, a self-aware person will ask themselves these questions: am I adequately restoring my energy? How can I exert and recharge my energy in a way that serves me? Of course, it's not just our introverted friends who suffer. During the lockdowns of the COVID-19 pandemic, our extroverted friends needed to be checked on. While introverts were relishing in more time to spend at home on their own, extroverts were losing all of their charge as they were restricted from all the things that fill them up: socialising, stimulating environments and large groups of people.

I don't want to sound like a bossy parent, but I want you to take the introversion versus extroversion thing seriously. Not because it's just another label you can slap on your chest, but because if you're aware of how to recharge and manage your energy, you'll have a shitload more of it to invest in the things that matter to you, including your manifestation practice.

IT'S TIME TO EXERCISE BETTER

My dad was a marathon runner. Not just your regular ol'
42.2 kilometres, though. He competed in the ultramarathons
in South Africa that were a torturous 89 kilometres. So as his
daughter, it seemed like a logical response for me to think that I'd
be able to pull off a similar feat. I'd never really understood the
runner's high that people went on about, but I pushed myself to
run because it was clearly in my blood.

I decided to enter myself in a half-marathon (ya know, baby
steps) and began training six months before the event. I followed
a training method that promised to have me comfortably
running 21.1 kilometres in time for the race, but each day that
I ran, I knew it wasn't for me. I didn't feel invigorated, I felt
completely depleted. My feet would pulsate and, in response,
I'd take magnesium and tell myself that running was all in the
mind, not in the body. During my weekly 15 kilometre run, I'd
be struggling, pushing and waiting impatiently for the addiction
to kick in – for the high to overcome me, for the euphoria to set

in – but it never did. On the day of the half-marathon, I organised for a bunch of friends to wait for me at the finish line. What an achievement it would be to complete my first half-marathon and have my nearest and dearest cheering me on!

As the race kicked off, hordes of people bolted in front of me. 'That's okay,' I told myself. 'You're running your own race. Stay in your own lane and get lost in the sound of your tunes.' (I'd curated the perfect running playlist.) So I did. But when I hit the 10-kilometre mark (roughly halfway), I felt a twinge in my right knee. 'It's all in your head,' I told myself. 'This isn't meant to be easy. Just keep running.' By the time I hit the 15-kilometre mark, I was hobbling but still technically running. I passed a St John Ambulance station and one of the paramedics started jogging beside me (let's be honest, it was a medium-paced walk) and suggested that I stop for a check-up. 'Sweetheart, your knee is swollen. I can tell just by looking at it. Please let me sit you down and check on it,' he pleaded. 'Nope, I've only got 6 kilometres to go. I have to finish this race. My friends are waiting for me,' I insisted. He ignored my stubborn moans and led/dragged me to the ambulance station, where he wrapped ice around my knee and told me that the best course of action was for me to be driven to the finish line. So that's what we did and I ended up at the finish line with crutches and my tail between my legs.

'Was this your first long-distance race? You don't really have the right body for running,' said my physio the next day. Before you get outraged by his comments on my physique, what he meant was that I wasn't made physically for the impact that running has on the body. All of my joints are extremely hyper-mobile, so when I run my entire body moves around like an elastic band, in particular my hips, knees and ankles. What the physio didn't say, but which I have since learned, is that I also don't have the energetic capacity for long-distance and endurance exercise. This isn't something that a doctor can diagnose you with, but after exercising for many years and trying different modalities such as CrossFit, spin classes, yoga, boxing, HIIT, circuit training, Pilates and soft-sand running, I discovered that anything enduring or high intensity depletes me of all of my energy and, in turn, leaves me constantly tired, makes my body gain and retain weight and affects my ability to sleep well. This took me years to come to terms with, because I love being active, I'm super competitive, we're told that exercise is vital to obtaining physical perfection and, well, I'm a sucker for an unachievable goal. You see, high-intensity exercise didn't just make me feel tired, the energy depletion it created made me unable to concentrate at work, too tired to socialise with friends, unable to focus on simple conversations and, without sounding super dramatic, rendered me unable to function as a normal human. No, I'm not a doctor or a trained professional in any capacity, but I can tell you that everyone has different energetic capacities when it comes to exercise, and a little self-awareness will show you what yours are. The most difficult thing is not working out what kind of exercise makes you feel good but coming to terms with the fact that what you enjoy might not always be the best thing for you, even if it's the perfect thing for someone else.

Exercise 14
HOW DO YOU EXERCISE?

I'm not going to take you through all the different types of exercise to curate a regimen that works for you (I'm not your bloody personal trainer), but I want you to answer the following questions to get curious about *why* you exercise, what benefit you get from it and if it's actually giving you energy or taking it away.

Jot down the answers to these questions in your self-awareness journal.

1. How often do I exercise?

2. Would I classify my choice of exercise as low, medium or high intensity?

3. How do I feel after I exercise?

4. What benefits do I experience from exercise?

5. What is my reason for exercising?

6. Does my choice of exercise energise me?

7. Do I feel depleted after I exercise?

If, like me, you've just realised the exercise that's been prescribed for years by women's magazines and fitness influencers isn't actually working for you and you're worried about what your gym buddies will say, I want you to think of it like this … You know how some people (me) love coriander, while others are so repulsed by it that they unnecessarily include their distaste for it in their dating profiles? Well, that's because the people who hate the best herb in the world are actually tasting something that resembles soap. Due to a variation in certain genes, their tastebuds are creating a completely different flavour profile to what coriander fanatics are experiencing. It's the same for people who feel incredible after high-intensity exercise. They'll tell you you're crazy (or lazy if they're feeling particularly insulting) for not enjoying running up mountains or lifting kettlebells over your head. They'll try and convince you that you're doing it wrong or that you should try their gym or this instructor or these shoes, but the truth is they're experiencing an after-exercise high that's totally different to yours. They can't relate to that feeling of utter exhaustion you get because they're tasting a delicious herb while you're eating soap. So please, learn from my years of trying to be my dad who ran marathons, my peers who aced CrossFit or my yogi friends who could tolerate vinyasa seven days a week, and get curious about how your energy feels after exercise and in the hours that follow.

I feel like I should put a caveat here and say I'm by no means telling you not to exercise. Exercise is vital to good health and I still move my body every day. I also want to emphasise that I'm not saying that you shouldn't feel like you're working hard *during* exercise – because of course you will if you do circuit training, trail running or any form of high-intensity exercise – but what you need to be aware of is how you feel *after* exercise. It should energise you. It should make you feel better, not worse, and if it's not, then it's time to try something new. You have to have an awareness of your energy to know when it feels good or when you feel depleted and figure out if exercise is affecting that. When we ignore what our energy is telling us, because it doesn't align with what we think we should be doing, we can find ourselves in burnout or energetic depletion.

WORK IT, BABY! BUT NOT TOO HARD

I'm going to say some controversial things over the next few paragraphs. It's going to make some of you angry (apologies in advance), some of you jealous (again, sorry) and others maybe even resentful. You see, I only work two–four hours a day. I'm not giving you a prescription for work success. I'm simply sharing how my work week looks. Some days, I don't work at all. Not because I don't have writing deadlines, an overflowing inbox or an endless to-do list, but because I'm so aware of my energy that I know if it's waning or feeling depleted in any way, my work productivity plummets so fast that it's easier to just call it day. Now, I'm fully aware that not everyone has this luxury. The fact that I work for myself allows flexibility that some of you might not have access to. But think of it like this: I'm using my work schedule to illustrate a greater concept (your energy) and how there are ways to be wiser about how you use it.

When I worked in publishing, I'd arrive at work as early as I could muster. If I had a big deadline, I'd come in as early as 7am. This would give me a couple of hours to get a big chunk of work done before the office filled up with chatter, coffee orders, recounts of the night before and lunch plans. Plus, I discovered in high school that my most productive and creative hours were long before the school bell rang or, in this case, the workday officially started. It's fair to say that throughout a standard workday (let's use nine–five as our definition of standard), there will be hours of the day where you feel most productive, and I guarantee it's not for those full eight hours. The same goes for creativity, tasks that require precision and, for me, I'd also factor in when I feel like I have the energy to engage with other people in meetings where I'm expected to dazzle. Throughout a standard day, you'll have moments where your energy peaks and plummets. Yes, a lot of this has to do with your hormones, the amount of caffeine and sugar you consume and how well you slept the night before, but even when all of that is taken out of the equation, you'll notice there are times throughout the day when you feel naturally elevated and when your energy slumps. Once you have an awareness and work with what you discover (i.e. accept and embody it), wow wee, you're going to find that not only are you more productive, but the quality of your work will be better because you're not forcing yourself to perform through an energy slump.

To this day, as a self-employed gal who works autonomously from home, I still start work at roughly 7am (depending on the season and whether or not I exercise in the morning or the afternoon). This is when my brain and physical energy are peaking and I know that the chapters I write between 7am and 11am will be far more useful than forcing myself to write later in the day. If you're looking at my writing schedule and think 'she's eager', it all comes down to genetics. This is why night owls find it near impossible to wake up early to watch the sunrise and early birds (like me) struggle to keep their eyes open past 10pm. It's about your chronotype. A chronotype is the natural inclination of your body to sleep at a certain time, but what many people don't know is that it also influences how you exercise, your appetite and how alert you are at certain periods throughout the day. Scientists usually describe two chronotypes: eveningness (night owls) and morningness (early birds). However, chronotypes fall on a spectrum, with most people lying somewhere in between. Just as with personality tests, there are several online chronotype tests you can do to determine where you sit. In the context of work, it's worth noting that although your chronotype is closely related to your circadian rhythm, which controls your daily sleep-wake cycle and releases melatonin in response to environmental cues such as light and temperature and can be 'trained' by adhering to a certain schedule, your chronotype is permanent. This means that a night owl may be able to force themselves to wake up at 7am for work, but they likely won't be alert or productive until later in the day. Conversely, an early bird will wake up bright and chipper, but their energy will start to wane by the late afternoon. Can you see why it's important that you have full awareness of how your energy shifts throughout your workday so that you can make the most of those hours of alertness and productivity? Great, let's jump into the next exercise.

Note: I know that not everyone works and this exercise might not relate to everyone's circumstances. (For example, I'm not sure doctors and nurses in emergency have the luxury to say, 'I'm only going to resuscitate people during the hours of 8–10am when I have the energy to do so.') Just answer the following questions as best you can.

Exercise 15

WHAT WORKS FOR YOU AT WORK?

Answer the following questions as honestly as you can. You may find that you're an energiser bunny and that you can work at the same pace all day without compromising your energy. Go you! Most of you, however, will notice there are certain hours of the day that you can utilise better.

Answer the following questions in your self-awareness journal:

1. How many hours a day do I work?

2. Of those hours, how many am I productive for?

3. What hours of the day am I most productive?

4. Are there hours of the day where I feel more creative? When are they?

5. When do I notice my energy slump?

6. Could stimulants such as caffeine and sugar be contributing to my slump?

7. How many hours of the day do I waste because I've run out of steam?

8. What would be the ideal workday hours for me?

Now, regardless of whether it's achievable for you or not, write down an ideal workday for you by assigning certain tasks to the hours where you're able to use your energy most wisely.

What I found most helpful about looking at my workday like this was that it filtered through to other areas of my life that required my energy too.

Exercise 16

LET'S APPLY THE HOURS RULE
TO THE REST OF YOUR LIFE

Keeping in mind your energy and how it wanes throughout the day, answer the following questions:

1. What time of the day do I prefer to socialise? For example, I have more energy in the earlier hours of the day so I try and organise catch-ups with friends in the morning or over lunch. I find I'm much more engaged in the conversation and can give them my full attention.

2. What time of the day do I prefer to exercise? Try not to factor in convenience but rather what makes your body feel better. For me, it's the morning but when I'm writing, I need those hours for productivity so I either exercise before I write or I move it to the afternoon and do something that I know won't tax my energy too much.

3. Are there times of the day that I find it easier to have deep and meaningful conversations or long phone chats with friends?

4. Are there times of the day that I find it easier to study or absorb new information? Again, I'm a morning person with

> this stuff, but I have friends who have the energy to focus on studying better once the sun has gone down. Find what works for you.
>
> These might seem like rudimentary questions, but can you see over time that if you're able to get curious about when your energy is good and can be used wisely that you're actually able to achieve more in your day in less time? Pretty cool, huh?

Rescheduling my workdays felt super indulgent at first, because we're so conditioned to believe that nine–five is considered a normal workday, but I've found that if I use my time wisely and stop working after those four hours are up, I have the capacity to get up and do the same again tomorrow. When I push myself to work all day and continue long past the hours I know my energy can handle (usually out of guilt), then it screws me up for the following day. Consistency and honouring when you need to rest or take time out are all a part of becoming more self-aware, which brings us to a vital part of any self-awareness practice around your own energy: rest.

THE IMPORTANCE OF REST

The practical side of me wants to tell you to rest because it's good for your productivity, creativity and general wellbeing. But the true gift of rest – the sublime value of full restoration, a space for your body to recharge, recalibrate and invigorate itself to alignment – is when you savour it like a tonic for the body. My introduction to deep rest was from a fellow yogi and Human Design facilitator, Emmie Rae, of The Daily Rest. She taught me that rest doesn't come with rules. You're not required to justify why you need it or why you've chosen to take it, and every time you rest, you empower everyone around you to indulge in the pleasure of rest too. And rest *is* a pleasure. For so long we've looked at rest as a task or even a sign of laziness, but if you can begin to view rest as an everyday indulgence that you look forward to and crave – that you know you deserve much like decadent dark chocolate or a fine red wine – then you'll be doing all sorts of wonderful favours to your energy, spirit and productivity.

Rest is not just sleep. We require much more rest than just six–eight hours of sleep at night. When we were biologically designed for slumber, we weren't doing much more than hunting, gathering, eating and maybe stargazing. Now we work crazy hours, squeeze in high-intensity exercise, do school drop-offs and pick-ups, cook three meals a day, keep the house tidy, fill up our social calendars, do the grocery runs, walk the dog, manage our finances, you get it … those few hours a night we crawl into our beds and shut our eyes is not enough to sustain our energy. It's time to start viewing rest as an integral part of a healthy lifestyle. It's as important for your vitality as nourishing nutrition and movement. It's as integral to your survival as water and just as hydrating for your cells.

So, what does rest look like?

Well, it will differ depending on your requirements. Here are a few different remedies for rest, ranging from most extreme to a quick catnap.

Lying in a dimly lit space with zero external stimulants

Dire circumstances call for dire remedies. When you've reached the point of burnout, just lying on the couch watching Netflix can still be too stimulating. The same has been said about listening to music. If you do want to play music, listen to relaxing instrumentals. Silence, if you can handle it, is the best remedy. If you fall asleep, that's great but you don't need to sleep to benefit from rest.

Avoiding stimulants such as coffee, alcohol and sugar

Anything that will stimulate your body and spike your energy will delay the body's ability to slip into a deeply restful state. Opt for relaxing herbal teas that contain calmatives such as chamomile, lavender and passionflower.

Considering easy-to-digest foods such as soups, congee and kitchari

When you're in a state of complete exhaustion, even making your digestive system work hard to process foods can be taxing on your body. Think simple, plant based and nothing that requires too much chewing.

Unplugging

This includes declining social engagements, forgoing strenuous exercise and perhaps even putting your phone on aeroplane mode (or at the very least on silent).

Restorative yoga at home

A deeply restorative yoga practice has you lying in each pose for at least 15 minutes supported by soft props and covered in blankets. No part of the practice should feel like it requires effort. It's an invitation for your body to completely surrender into deep relaxation.

Deep belly breathing

If you're experiencing anxiety or finding it difficult to drop into a restful state even though you're completely burnt out, the quickest way to drop into a parasympathetic state is through your breath. Take ten deep breaths in through your nose, right into the pit of your belly, and then exhale slowly out through your mouth. After ten breaths, you'll find your whole system begins to calm down.

Yoga nidra meditation

If you search my name on the Insight Timer app, you'll find a yoga nidra meditation narrated by yours truly to guide you into a yogic sleep. If you're not familiar with yoga nidra, it's a state of deep rest that's usually instructed by a guided meditation. It induces a state of consciousness between awake and asleep so while you remain awake during the practice, your body can experience deep relaxation.

Less screen time

Bingeing on a Netflix series can seem like a good way to rest (and when you're just tired, I'll allow it), but when your nervous system is fried, watching a crime thriller or even a sad movie is not doing your energy levels any favours. Your body doesn't know the difference between real danger and perceived danger on a TV, so I'd suggest either watching a beautiful nature doco or turning off the TV instead.

Taking a social media detox

PSA – you don't need to announce you're doing it, just do it. Scrolling through your social media apps is hardly a calming activity, so take a few days off and notice how it affects your nervous system.

Organising takeaway to take the pressure off cooking

When your body is in overwhelm and exhaustion, eliminating unnecessary tasks can make a huge difference. Getting takeaway for a couple of nights, combined with the pointers above, can feel like a mini holiday for your nervous system.

Slowing everything down

There's no need to rush through life. Look at your calendar and remove anything that's not urgent, move through your everyday tasks at a slower pace, savour every mouthful when you eat and, if you're a fast talker like me, be conscious of the speed at which you communicate.

Napping

I'm not a napper – I can't do it unless I'm jet-lagged or very sick – but if you have the luxury of being able to nap in the day and your body is telling you that you need to, then do it! Don't feel guilty, look at it as a gift to yourself.

Getting horizontal

Lie on the grass, lie on the couch, lie on the floor under your desk. Even if it's just for 20 minutes, it will allow your body time to decompress and recharge.

If you only drink water once you're thirsty, you're already dehydrated. The same applies to rest. There's no sense in waiting until you're depleted and exhausted before taking the time to incorporate rest into your life. You need to enjoy rest as a preventative measure and tonic to help you maintain your energy levels throughout the day.

Here's what I do to incorporate rest into every day:

★ I block out time in my calendar for rest, just as I would for an appointment or a work task.
★ During that allocated time slot, I might do a 20-minute yoga nidra or simply lie down on the floor with an eye pillow over my eyes.
★ If I know I have a particularly stressful week of work or will be working longer hours than I know my energy can

sustain, I incorporate a restorative yoga session into my week.

★ I ensure I have at least four nights free a week where I don't have social commitments. For some of you that might sound excessive, but I know that's what my system needs.

★ Most importantly, I drop the guilt around rest. If I can enjoy and savour rest, I find it ten times more rewarding.

If your life is busier than mine and you have little ones running around, you may feel that finding time to rest is impossible. If this is you, I want you to reframe how you currently enjoy the time you do have to yourself. Is it spent scrolling through social media? Is it spent running around like a headless chook? Could you slow down the process? Are you scheduling in social arrangements that you feel obligated to attend, rather than what you feel you're energetically capable of? Are you trying to maintain your energy levels with stimulants? Have you taken ten deep belly breaths today? Do it with the kids – I'm sure they'll love it! If you have time to binge on the new season of your favourite TV show, you have time to rest.

If you work full time and you're wondering how to incorporate rest into your day, ensure you take your one-hour lunch break. Out of the office if possible. Spend 20 minutes enjoying your food and the next 40 minutes resting. Put down your phone and do a guided yoga nidra or listen to some Tibetan sound bowls through your headphones and breathe into your belly. By the time you get back to work, you'll be feeling recharged for the afternoon and in a far more sustainable way than getting your buzz from that 3pm coffee and cake.

Exercise 17

HOW DO YOU REST?

Grab your self-awareness journal and let's start working out how you can incorporate rest into your day.

Answer the following questions:

《 How do I currently feel about the idea of resting?

《 Do I actively incorporate rest into my day?

《 What does rest look like for me?

《 How can I rest more?

If you don't take adequate time to rest, I want you to try it for just one week as an experiment. Start with 20 minutes of rest in the middle of the day (if you can, otherwise wherever you can get it) and get curious about how it makes you feel. Eventually (if possible), see if you can work yourself up to 60 minutes.

WHEN YOUR ENERGY GETS STUCK

I'm not about to give you a lecture on physics, because I'm absolutely not qualified (just ask my Year Eight science teacher), but I'll introduce you to a law of physics known as the conservation of energy. This principle states that energy can't be created or destroyed, BUT it can be altered. I believe that for the purposes of self-awareness, the simplest way to understand energy is through our physical and emotional senses. In *Make It Happen*, I wrote a lot about energy in terms of our vibrational frequency and how we can alter and move energy through having an emotional release such as crying, listening to music that provokes a feeling and letting anger out by punching a pillow or screaming cathartically. We can also shift energy through physically moving the body by going for a run, dancing around the kitchen to Beyoncé or any other form of movement that gets energy flowing freely through your body. We also learned that we can move energy by shifting our environment, from cleaning the house to rearranging furniture or moving office spaces. These are all palpable shifts in energy. We can feel the energetic transformation almost as if it was tangible. In Sanskrit, we call it *prana*, our life-force energy. In traditional Chinese culture, this life-force energy is referred to as *qi*. Either way, it's a physical and emotional feeling – perhaps subtle, perhaps palpable – that we can feel is either flowing through us or, alternatively, is stuck or blocked. If we go back to physics for a brief moment, the principle of energy conservation tells us that energy can exist in a closed system in which the energy is held or bound, or it can exist in an open system in which the energy flows. Uncontained energy can cause a system to become frenetic or fragmented. Depleted energy can cause a system to collapse. This is science, folks, and the energy that flows through you is no different. So, what causes a closed energy system within us? And what's the result of blocked energy? Well, let me tell you a tale …

The cure for writer's block? A happy ending

There are certain fantasies that a budding writer allows themselves to indulge in when they have a new writing project. For me, it's always been about creating the ultimate writing space. The reverie might start small and achievable, like a redo of my home office – a new chair, an oversized wall planner, a few cute pieces of decor, some coloured Post-its, an hourglass, a new notepad. Sometimes, the fantasy dares to venture outside and takes me to a local cafe where every morning I write away the hours while nibbling on croissants and sipping on English breakfast tea (who am I kidding? It's coffee). In this particular fantasy, strangers start conversations with me because they're so in awe of the fact that I'm a writer. In the acknowledgements section of my first book, I'll write, 'I couldn't have written this bestseller without the inspiration of my local cosy cafe with their buttery, flaky pastries and endless pots of tea (read: coffee).' My ultimate writing fantasy ventures a little further abroad, or at the very least to an Australian rainforest bungalow, where said writing project practically writes itself. The criteria for this oasis is simple: remote, quaint, idyllic, inspirational and ideally with the sweet melodic tunes of local birds. Well, that's one scenario, anyway.

Any writer would agree that the idea of removing yourself from your everyday routine and environment is a foolproof recipe for the state of flow that creatives chase. How could one NOT pen a literary masterpiece when perched in a Parisian sidewalk cafe, an Airbnb on a remote Greek island or tucked away in a log cabin in the middle of the Australian bush? Well, with more than 15 years of experience as a writer under my belt and two books written in less than two years, I can tell you that, much like a bad hair day will follow you around no matter your location, so will a writer's ultimate nemesis – writer's block.

When I landed my first book deal in 2018, I was given an eight-week deadline to write the manuscript. 'Fuck it,' I thought. 'Who knows if I'll ever get an opportunity like this again?' I frantically googled writer's retreat, writer's cabin, famous writing destinations and the ultimate writing spots. Turns out, there are a bunch of other writers out there that also think the answer to locating their creativity and productivity is found very far away from their actual home, because there were a lot of options! I settled on a villa in Ubud, Bali. I could have an entire villa to myself with a pool, daily delivered cold-pressed Jamu and green juices, a yoga school walking distance away and a strip of healthy cafes at my disposal. I booked a ten-day getaway, confident that I would get more done in ten days in Ubud than the entire eight-week deadline back home in Sydney.

By day three in my Bali oasis, I'd consumed enough Jamu juice that my skin was turning a subtle shade of turmeric, enjoyed morning swims, lunchtime swims and sunset swims, created a beautiful morning yoga routine, discovered the best dinner spots in walking distance and written a whopping three paragraphs of my manuscript. In case you require context for what's productive when writing a book in eight weeks, let me tell you that one paragraph a day is not a milestone you aim for. It was official: I'd hit the dry bank of distress known as writer's block, even while living my best life in Bali. I've heard many well-respected writers make good cases for why writer's block is just another procrastination tool used to stall what ultimately is their quest for perfection, but I also read an article in *The New Yorker* that made me feel like it was absolutely a thing and I suffered from it constantly. According to this article, the term was first coined in the 1940s by psychiatrist Edmund Bergler who, after two decades of studying writers who suffered from 'neurotic inhibitions of productivity' (have you ever felt more seen in your life?), found that the remedy for these so-called blockages was some good old-fashioned therapy. Bergler's theory fit my particular crime, so I felt confident blaming my inability to write on the dreaded block. I'd just begun writing my first non-fiction book in which I was attempting to tell really personal stories, and I was paralysed by the pressure of finding the perfect way to do so while not slipping into old wounds. Therapy was exactly what I needed.

After unsuccessfully googling 'How to cure writer's block' and failing to get an appointment with my therapist in time, I reached out to a few friends who frequented Bali for advice around a therapy substitute, alternative treatment or whether anybody could point me in the direction of an *Eat, Pray, Love* medicine man. While I was devastated to hear of Ketut's passing two years prior, I was given a bunch of recommendations for a breathwork circle that was held every Thursday a few kilometres from where I was staying. I'd attempted breathwork once before, but the experience didn't feel quite 'right'. I remember hyperventilating and consequently having a panic attack while my friend was contorting her body beside me like she'd been possessed by a poltergeist. I found myself thinking, 'What the fuck is this madness?' When it was over, I turned to my possessed pal who responded with, 'How fucking cool was that?' Huh? I've since learned that she'd done a proper breathwork circle before that was facilitated by a trained professional and her body contortion was one of the benefits of the practice. So, while slightly traumatised by my first breathwork experience, I'd always remained intrigued. And at this point, I was desperate. I'd entered day four of my writing dry spell and as I sat down to attempt paragraph four, I instead booked myself in for the breathwork circle that afternoon.

If you're wondering why I thought breathing would help my 'neurotic inhibitions of productivity', as Bergler put it, let me tell you the touted benefits of the practice. Just to be clear, the breathwork I'm referring to is a particular form of controlled breath. There are lots of different breathing practices across many different traditions. In the yogic tradition, *pranayama* is used to describe a variety of breathing practices that are usually combined with a yoga or meditation practice and serve different purposes. Everything from a slow, rhythmic breath such as *nadi shodhana* (alternate nostril breathing) to switch on your parasympathetic nervous system and relieve stress to *kapalabhati* (breath of fire), a rapid breathing technique to detoxify the body and sharpen the mind. The breathwork I was embarking on was an amalgamation of different breathing practices that releases the exhale rather than forcing or controlling it. It's believed that, when performed correctly in a safe and facilitated environment, this rapid breathing pattern in and out of the mouth with no pauses can alter your state of consciousness without the use of drugs. When in this state, studies have shown that it can help reduce symptoms of insomnia, depression, PTSD and anxiety, and it's also the quickest way to change your state of being and point of view. Google also told me that breathwork is incredible at unlocking creativity, accessing your subconscious and moving through psychological impasses.

Hallelujah! Who needs therapy when they can just breathe their way out of neurotic inhibitions? Note: plenty of people need therapy (including myself).

When you book a treatment or service in Bali, you can't always be sure of what you're walking into, but when I arrived at the address of the breathwork circle, I was pleasantly surprised. The circle was held in a beautiful luxury resort in Ubud where tourists were enjoying their stress-free holidays reading by the pool, ordering cocktails from the bar and making their way to an afternoon yoga class. A beautiful local woman led me to the outdoor pavilion where the breathwork circle would take place. I have to admit, I was nervous. My last experience hadn't been positive and I couldn't get the image of my friend's claw-like hands out of my head.

At the pavilion, I was greeted by a Japanese woman who instructed me to get comfortable while we waited for the others. She led me to a yoga mat with supportive props including a yoga bolster, several pillows, a couple of blankets and a silk eye pillow. Perhaps this was going to be 90 minutes of restorative bliss? I lay there in anticipation trying to relax, but I could feel my heart jumping out of my chest. Before long, ten of us were lying down comfortably in a circle. Our facilitator instructed us to sit up to face each other and introduce ourselves. We were given two minutes each to say our name, where we were from, what our experience of breathwork was and why we were there. To my surprise, most people were regulars who lived in Bali or were staying for an extended period of time and had been attending these circles weekly. Each person relayed their reasons for being there, ranging from looking for a natural high to clearing PTSD from trauma. No matter our reason for attending that day, we were told that whatever the body wishes to release will be released and sometimes what surfaces throughout the session will be nothing like your original intention.

Our facilitator spent 20 minutes teaching us the specific breathing technique that we'd be using and reiterated the importance of practising under supervision, which kind of freaked me out. What type of breathing was too dangerous to practise without supervision? As often happens when I get nervous, I had a sudden urge to pee. As we reached the end of our breath training and were instructed to get comfortable, as we'd be lying there for the next 45 minutes, I had that tale-as-old-as-time predicament – do I go to the toilet or just hope that the urge to wet myself will pass? All around me, the room began to erupt in an array of uncomfortable sounds. There was quiet sobbing coming from one corner reminiscent of a whimpering puppy, an inconsolable tantrum coming from another corner and then next to me a woman, who'd appeared timid during the introduction, was convulsing and contorting much like my friend had done and letting out what could only be described as painful howls. As I continued with my breath, determined to feel something other than an urgency to empty my bladder, the facilitator reassured us that everything being experienced by participants was very normal and just an indication that there was energy in the body that needed to be released so that the body could heal. The only thing my body wanted to release was pee (sorry, too graphic?), so I dashed to the loo, felt that incomparable sensation of an empty bladder and then raced straight back to my mat and continued with the cyclical mouth breathing.

It took me 15 minutes to get back into the rhythm, drag my focus away from the cacophony of 'releases' happening around me and allow all of my attention to be on my own body. As I finally began to relax, feeling the breath become more easeful and less like I was going to hyperventilate, I noticed a strange (given the circumstances) sensation sweep through the lower half of my body. Well, my groin if I'm being specific, which I think I have to be in order to convey exactly what was happening in this moment. The rhythmic nature of nothing but my breath was making me rather, ahem, aroused. Surely not. I found it hard to orgasm at the best of times, let alone with zero physical stimulation and among a group of wailing strangers. The facilitator interjected, 'Allow whatever comes up to come up and surrender to the experience. The body will release energy in the best way it knows how.' Turns out, my body was intent on releasing energy through sexual arousal. Plot twist! As I lay there, still undecided if I was going to take this experience to its ultimate climax, articles about tantric breathing and Kundalini energy flooded back into my mind. Was I having an energetic orgasm? I didn't even have to think sexy thoughts to intensify the pulsating wave of energy that was culminating not only in my nether regions, but through my entire body.

We were told we only had five minutes to go and a part of me slipped into panic mode, worried I wasn't going to see this orgasm through. I drowned out the commotion of the rest of the room, brought all of my focus inward, intensified my breath and rolled my body ever so slightly to the right and there it was – the crescendo I'd been building up to for the past 45 minutes (minus that bolt to the bathroom). My toes curled, my back arched and I bit my lip in an attempt to mute the moan that was dying to escape from my mouth, but I'm pretty sure the contortionist beside me heard my whimper as my entire body flooded with a warmth, a pleasure, an energetic pulsation I'd never experienced before. We were told to slowly bring ourselves back to our normal breath and remain lying down until we felt it was time to return to a seated position. As I lay there, still shaking yet completely surrendered, in no position to be able to peel myself back into a seat, I finally understood the French term '*la petite mort*' – translated in English to 'the little death' – which describes that moment post-orgasm. I did feel as if I'd died and subsequently been reborn.

I chose not to contribute to the sharing circle post-breathing, because how do you tell a group of strangers that you just experienced the most intense orgasm of your life? But the general theme of what was shared among the group was that they recalled memories, conversations and feelings throughout their life that were being released through the aforementioned wailing, contortions etc. and that they now felt lighter, freer, more satisfied. *That* I could relate to. But what of my writer's block? Instead of tapping away at my keyboard all this time, should I have been tapping away at my clitoris instead? (My whole teenage life I aspired to be Carrie Bradshaw. I think I may have just realised that dream.)

As I was driven back to the villa past expansive rice fields and picturesque mountain scapes, I could feel there was a new life force inside of me. After a dip in the pool to cool off what had been an unexpectedly steamy day, I pulled out my laptop to prepare to pen my masterpiece, but nothing came (except for me a couple of hours prior – sorry, it was there so I had to take it). Truth be told,

I was exhausted. I made myself an early dinner, tucked myself into bed and had one of the deepest sleeps I'd had since arriving in Bali. The next morning when I woke up, I made myself a pot of tea and sat in front of the laptop. That day, I wrote triple what I'd written since my arrival, and although words weren't pouring out of me like a flowing tap, my 'drain' had definitely been unclogged. There was an ease to my writing that hadn't been there prior, which I think was due to me getting out of my head and back into my body. There were two major things I learned during that breath circle and even though they were quite separate in nature, they complemented each other in this instance.

1. The best cure for writer's block is an exertion or release of pent-up stress and energy. In this particular instance it was released through orgasm, but I'm sure it won't surprise you to know that every time I get writer's block I don't bring myself to climax. Instead, I remember the impact of releasing energy and go for a walk, do a yoga class or run on the beach with a friend's dog. Of course, this applies to any type of energy blocks, not just the writing variety.

2. The breath revolutionises orgasm. In fact, there are breath orgasm workshops where a bunch of women gather in a circle and, through different breathing techniques instructed by a sex therapist or tantric practitioner, all come to orgasm. Yes, everyone in the room at the same time. If you've never connected your breath with sexual arousal, I highly recommend giving it a go.

Breathing is just one of many ways to encourage energy to flow freely through the body. We discussed earlier that physical movement and environmental changes can assist with this, but I believe breathing is the most accessible. Even just five minutes of conscious deep breathing can alter the state of not just your nervous system, but also your heart rate, blood pressure, monkey mind and emotional impulses. When your energy gets blocked or stagnant, the breath encourages movement back into an otherwise sedentary state.

MANIFESTATION REMINDER

It's believed that the energy and high-vibrational frequency that's emitted by the body during orgasm is the perfect foundation for your intentions to bloom. Many manifestation teachers preach intention setting or visualising your manifestation during or immediately after climax.

Causes of blocked energy

When your energy is flowing freely through the body, your mind is open and clear, you feel light, expansive and motivated, and time feels spacious. When your energy is blocked, it can manifest physically, mentally and emotionally. Your thoughts become fixed and narrow-minded. Your mind feels foggy and unable to find clarity. Emotions feel overwhelming and nonsensical or you may even feel numb and detached. You possibly find it hard to feel balanced, honour boundaries and fully comprehend what you need to feel satisfied. Here are some of the causes of energy blocks:

★ Stress and trauma can cause mental and emotional processes to shut down, causing a closed system within your energetic field.
★ Limiting beliefs can get in the way of what you believe is possible for you, causing a block to where you're able to direct your energy.
★ When you have a lack of faith in yourself or the universe, you slip into fear and when you're in fear, your energy can become paralysed.
★ Suppressing and ignoring your feelings causes a build-up of unexpressed emotions in the body, blocking a clear pathway for energy to flow. See Chapter 4 for how to effectively process and express emotions.

One of the pioneers of body psychotherapy, Wilhelm Reich, theorised that we block our own energy to defend against unwanted feelings or impulses. He described these blocks as 'the physical instrument of emotional repression' and saw blocking energy as an adaptive strategy to manage life's challenges.

Exercise 18
GETTING TO KNOW YOUR ENERGY

I believe that being acutely aware of your own energy is key, because only you'll be able to recognise when energy is blocked or stuck, and only you are capable of altering your energy into a state of flow. So, let's have a look at some ways of understanding your own energy better. Contemplate the following:

1. Become aware of your thoughts. Are your thoughts fixed and inflexible or are they open-minded and adaptable?

2. Throughout the day, check in with your breath. Is it shallow and frenetic? Is it slow and deep? Do you hold your breath?

3. Check in with your body. Do you feel grounded and stable? Do you feel agitated and kinetic? Does your body need to move? Or does your body need to rest?

4. Become aware of your emotions. Are you adequately processing and expressing them? Are you suppressing and ignoring them? Can you feel your emotions? Or do you feel like you're dissociating?

5. Do you feel like your energy is your own? Or do you feel like your energy is demanded by others?

6. When you're around certain people and in certain environments, does your energy expand and feel free and light? Or does your energy constrict and feel tight and heavy?

BOUNDARIES

I'm a lazy feminist. Not because I don't believe in the cause, but because I let the passionate feminists fight the fight for me and I just ride on the coat-tails of all their hard work #guilty. However, there is one little feminist issue that does get my knickers in a knot: when a woman is labelled as difficult or a bitch for having boundaries and being assertive (i.e. asking for what she wants). Men do it all the bloody time without question. They're never labelled as a bastard, disruptive or difficult simply for saying no.

Boundaries are so sexy, truly! Once I started using them, I saw how freaking coveted they were. People began complimenting my use of them as if they were a new designer handbag after which they'd been lusting. Even the people who I'd put boundaries in place for respected me and my use of them, because it gave them permission to do the same. So if boundaries are such a precious commodity and are available to everyone, why do so many of us struggle to have any?

What are boundaries?

Put simply, personal boundaries are the lines we draw for ourselves in terms of our level of comfort around others. These boundaries could be to do with physical contact, verbal interactions or regarding your own personal space. They could be emotional, physical, energetic, sexual, professional or material and they could even be around your time. The tricky thing about boundaries is that there is no rule book. Everyone's boundaries are different, and most people don't know what theirs are, which means boundaries are often getting crossed with neither party able to take responsibility. Often, for me, I'll become aware of a boundary only once it's been crossed. This is quite normal. It's then up to me to set a clear boundary in the future and this comes down to clear communication.

How to set clear boundaries:

★ Name and recognise your feelings. Ask yourself, 'How do I feel around this person? Why am I feeling this way? How can I feel safer? What would need to change?'

★ Communicate your boundary to others. As much as it pains me to admit, people aren't mind-readers. Communicating a boundary can set the stage for the conversation or interaction and where you're willing to go with it.

★ Recognise other people's boundaries and show gratitude for their setting them. People who have trouble with setting boundaries usually have trouble respecting others' boundaries. Be conscious of this. If you're not sure of another person's boundary, ask them.

★ Boundary setting is an act of self-care. Putting your energetic, emotional and physical comfort first is a beautiful expression of self-love. Own it!

★ Learn to say 'no thank you' without giving an explanation or apology. We'll talk about the art of this simple phrase before the end of this chapter.

★ Check in with your personal core values. We set them in Chapter 4. Are they being compromised? If so, it's time to pop up a boundary.

★ Work out the consequences in advance. I like this one because if I know a situation or person is going to make me feel resentful without a certain boundary in place, it's absolutely not worth it to me in the long run.

I've found that the better you get at setting your own boundaries, the easier it is to recognise other people's boundaries.

How to recognise someone else's boundaries:

★ Read their body language. A self-aware and emotionally intelligent person will be able to recognise if someone is uncomfortable. If they're pulling away from you, unable to make eye contact or crossing their arms in order to protect themselves, it's likely an indication that a boundary has been crossed.

★ No means no. I feel that this is pretty self-explanatory, but if someone tells you no, believe them. It takes a lot for certain people to say no, so respect that and don't make it your mission to turn it into a yes.

★ Respect their requests. This is the same vein as the previous point. If someone has communicated a request to you, respecting it is honouring their boundaries.

★ If you're not sure, just ask. I do this all the time, and people bloody love it. It can be hard to communicate a personal boundary, but if someone invites you to share your boundaries, it's such a gift. Give that gift to someone else.

Exercise 19

WHAT ARE YOUR BOUNDARIES?

It's not likely that you're going to know all of your boundaries off the top of your head, but there's no harm in starting to get curious about what your boundaries are around certain things. Grab your self-awareness journal and write down some of your personal boundaries for the following categories:

1. Emotional boundaries – these are boundaries that protect your own emotional wellbeing.

2. Physical boundaries – these are boundaries that impact your personal space.

3. Energetic boundaries – these are boundaries that deplete you of energy.

4. Sexual boundaries – these are boundaries that protect your safety and respect your needs sexually.

5. Material boundaries – these are boundaries that protect your personal belongings.

6. Time boundaries – these are boundaries for the use and misuse of your time.

Somewhere along the line, boundaries were thought to be selfish because they require you to put your own needs before others'. Like that's a bad thing?! The point of boundaries is to protect yourself from your energetic, emotional and physical reserves being drained, and who can fault you for that? No one, nor should they! Boundary setting, however, does require a certain level of assertiveness.

Be assertive. Be, be assertive!

We've already covered the fact that assertion, especially when it comes from women, is often labelled as bitchy or difficult, and it's the reason why many women avoid it at all costs. By the dictionary definition, being assertive is about having a confident and forceful personality, but I believe being assertive is also about asking for what you want in a calm and confident manner, without being aggressive or confrontational. This sounds pretty gender-neutral to me.

I haven't always been an assertive little (lazy) feminist with clear boundaries – far from it! I actually used to be a bit of a doormat.

However, my mother began training me from quite a young age to be more assertive, knowing that I was going to meet plenty of people throughout my lifetime who would walk all over me if they got the opportunity. I can actually hear her right now when I would cower under her skirt as a six-year-old: 'Jord, you've got to be more assertive!' She would give me little tests in order to strengthen my ability to ask for what I wanted. It started with placing my own order when we went to a cafe, which then led me to confronting bullies at school and eventually asking for a promotion when I started working in publishing. 'People aren't mind-readers,' she would say. 'You have to ask for what you want. If you don't stand up for yourself, no one else will.' Sage advice. Little did she know that my assertion training from as young as six years old would result in a woman who today gets complimented on her assertiveness and clear boundary setting. Thanks, Mum.

How to be assertive (not aggressive)

Assertive and aggressive are two different adjectives, but they're often mistaken for one another. I think the misdemeanour occurs because there's so much fear associated with being assertive that we take it to the extreme in order for our assertion to not be misconstrued, and it ends up sounding aggressive. Been there, done that. So, let's have a look at how you can be assertive while remaining cool, calm and collected.

Get clarity around what you need to say

This is a vital step in being assertive. You need to be clear on what you're being assertive about. What's your intention? What do you need to achieve? If you can get clarity around the issue first, you're more likely to communicate it effectively.

Practise good communication

The next chapter speaks of this in depth, so you have no excuses. Clear communication, which includes listening, is the key to being successfully assertive. It's about recognising that there's another person (or people) in the conversation. Also, ensure that your body language is congruent with your words. If you're expressing that you need something by a certain deadline but you're not making eye contact, your shoulders are slumped and you're fidgeting with your hands, it's not likely your attempt at being assertive will be taken seriously. A great psychological hack is that when you stand tall and make eye contact, your mind and words will tend to follow what your body does.

Personalise it

Frame your communication from your own perspective rather than someone else's. This means saying things like 'I feel' rather than 'you make me feel'.

Avoid accusations

It always helps when being assertive to remember that we're all human and most people will act from a place of fear, avoidance or defensiveness if they feel threatened. So recognise their vulnerability and try to be empathetic, but ...

Practise cognitive empathy

We spoke about this in Chapter 4. Cognitive empathy is when

you intellectually put yourself in someone else's shoes without having to take on all of their feelings. This, of course, will depend on who you're conversing with, but when being assertive, I've found that leaving big emotions out of it is a sure-fire way to ensure it doesn't become aggressive.

Recognise when you're not getting anywhere and let it go

Sometimes you'll be assertive and you won't get the desired outcome. It's important to recognise when to take a breath and let it go. This isn't about admitting defeat but rather about accepting that a particular tactic isn't penetrating. When we keep forcing a matter that isn't being received properly is when we can become aggressive or defensive.

The two 'NO' rules

Jim Carrey tried to convince us all to become a 'yes man' (or woman) in the movie *Yes Man*, and I see the validity in saying 'yes' to things that you'd usually dismiss without a second thought. But I believe one of our biggest misdemeanours (especially for women) is actually our inability to say 'no' and stick to it. If you're a bit of a people pleaser (FYI, most of us are), you'll likely find yourself trying desperately to keep someone else happy at the expense of your own emotions, energy or time. This is where learning to say 'no' in a healthy and assertive way becomes your greatest secret weapon. But there are two rules when it comes to saying no and not coming across as aggressive or difficult.

1. **Start with a hard NO.** By this, I mean if you start with a soft 'no' or an 'I'm not sure' when you really are bloody sure, it gives people room to start convincing you otherwise. If you cave in on that first 'no', it makes it ten times harder to come back later and be like 'actually, you know what? NO!' A hard 'no' if you're not used to saying 'no' might feel uncomfortable at first, but it will save you so much time and energy in the long run. However, it's really important that you know that 'no' isn't an aggressive word, especially when you use it like you do in rule number two.

2. **Learn to say 'no, thank you'.** Saying 'no' is not a defiant or aggressive response, it's just one of two responses to a yes or no question. Popping 'thank you' on the end is recognition that you're not saying no from a place of negativity, but rather from a place of asserting your right to a response of your choice.

The trick to a successful hard 'no' and a 'no, thank you' is not offering an explanation, apology or excuse. When you start trying to make excuses for why you're saying no to make the other person feel more comfortable, it starts to make you sound less confident in your choice.

Here are some other ways you can say no that ensure you're being firm and unapologetic while still remaining kind and polite:

★ 'No, but thank you for asking.'
★ 'Not now, but maybe next time.'

★ 'I can't say yes at this point but let me get back to you.'
★ 'Thank you for thinking of me, but I'll have to pass.'
★ 'Thank you for asking, but I just don't have the energetic capacity at this time.'

What do you think? Not too scary, is it? I have some homework for you ...

Exercise 20
PRACTISING BEING ASSERTIVE

If the idea of being assertive makes you drip with sweat, I want you to step outside your comfort zone and give some of my tips for being assertive a go this week.

Also, practise saying 'no, thank you' as often as you can. Remember a 'no' needn't come with an explanation or an apology. If you feel one sneaking up on you, bite your tongue and see how impactful a simple 'no, thank you' actually is.

You could spend a long time getting clear on what all of your boundaries are, but if you don't actually implement them, they're redundant. I had an incident this week where I consciously knew my boundary was about to be crossed and I let it happen anyway, knowing I would inevitably suffer the consequences. That shit's on me! I'm only human after all, but boundaries are only effective when we can embody them and implement them. It takes practice, stepping outside your comfort zone and sometimes it means not getting a favourable reaction out of people, but once you start asserting your own boundaries, not only will people be so incredibly envious that you know what your boundaries are and you adhere to them, but they'll also respect the hell out of you too.

ENERGY AND THE THREE STEPS OF SELF-AWARENESS

Your energy is in a constant state of flux. If you're not in tune with your own energy, it can go from free-flowing and fancy-free to stuck, stagnant and blocked without you even realising. Having an acute sense of self-awareness and a solid understanding of your own energetic capacity will enable you to be hyper-aware of when your energy is being affected so that you're able to incorporate more rest, pull back on your exercise routine or rejig your work schedule accordingly.

Step 1: Curiosity

We got curious about your current energy levels, but it's likely that you'll constantly need to be checking in with your energy levels daily and adjusting where necessary. I know that I have to adjust my routine daily in order to honour the energy I have on any particular day. If you're looking for some extracurricular lines of enquiry around your energetic self, you might like to look into the following:

- ★ What are the tell-tale signs that your energy is waning? Catching a depletion in energy before you're fully depleted will prevent total burnout.
- ★ Do certain people, environments or conversations affect your energy? Why?

Step 2: Acceptance

You may discover that you don't have as much energy as you thought you did. This might come as a major disappointment and if you're anything like me, you'll search for ways to increase your energy levels, desperate to keep up with the energiser bunnies. Sure, there are some great natural remedies for boosting your energy – cutting out certain stimulants will also help – but at a certain point, accepting your own energetic capability and capacity for what it is will serve you so much better in the long run. You see, once you can honour your unique energetic make-up and stop living as if you have the energy of an 18-year-old after their second Red Bull, you'll actually find that you have more energy than ever before.

When it comes to your boundaries, I believe the biggest struggle for people is accepting that it's okay to have them. When we have no boundaries, it's because we're putting other people's emotions, energy and needs above our own. It can take a lot to accept that you are your priority, but hopefully the further into this book you get, the more you realise that putting yourself first isn't selfish, it's simply creating a more authentic and aligned version of you.

Step 3: Embodiment

Someone who's able to be the embodiment of their true energetic self will:

- ★ Check in with their energy each morning and decide how they'll make good use of their energy that day.
- ★ Adjust their exercise routine to one that makes them feel good.
- ★ Set up their work calendar to make the most of their productive hours.
- ★ Take rest often.
- ★ Not feel obligated to attend social engagements at the expense of their own energy.
- ★ Be conscious of when to move their body in order to shift stuck or stagnant energy.
- ★ Execute clear boundaries.
- ★ Be comfortable saying 'no, thank you' without giving an excuse, apology or explanation.

Your energy is one of your most precious assets. Use it wisely, conserve it where you can and recharge it often. If you take away only one thing from this chapter, let it be the ability to celebrate rest because it really is the secret to sustained energy.

CHAPTER 6

Communication

If I could rejig the high school education system, I would change a multitude of things. First of all, I'd get rid of trigonometry. Tan, cos, sin? Never used them, not once! Perhaps teaching, 'Don't get a TAN in the sun COS you will SINge your beautiful youthful skin,' would've been more beneficial for my 15-year-old sun-obsessed self to learn. Then, I'd tackle sex education. Instead of focusing so heavily on contraception – which is important, but also something most teenagers are heavily invested in getting right (nobody wants to feature on *Teen Mom*) – how about focusing on consent and, here's something revolutionary, pleasure?! Also taking priority in my complete overhaul of the education system would be communication, because it really does lay the foundation for everything once you leave school. Doesn't it blow your mind that we're not taught how to converse clearly, speak with intention, listen patiently and signal understanding and support with not just our words, but our body language too?

I happen to have a natural talent for communication, which is bloody lucky for me, but I've also been swanning around on Earth long enough to know that communication isn't a one-way street. Whether you're in conversation with one person, a group of people or communicating to millions of people through a book, TED Talk or presidential campaign, having an acute awareness of how you're received is just as important as how you deliver your message. In this chapter, we're going to explore the different types of communication and what type of communicator you are, the error of miscommunication, the power of silence, why you're likely smarter than school had you believe you were and the underrated beauty of body language. I'm also going to help you figure out what your strengths and weaknesses are when it comes to communication, because how you converse, listen and receive information is a direct reflection of how you interact with the world and, in turn, how it interacts with you. Powerful stuff, right? Self-awareness, of course, is crucial to effective communication. Once you have an understanding of your personality, values, thoughts, feelings, desires, boundaries and behaviours (which you'll have by the end of this book), you'll be able to not only communicate your own needs, but also understand the needs of others.

TYPES OF COMMUNICATION

Before you start making wild proclamations about being a terrible communicator, I think it's important to be aware that communication is so much more than verbally conversing with someone. I believe communication is best explained when broken down into six main categories. You may excel at all of them, but you'll likely find that you have more strengths in one category than another. Let's explore them and then you can decide where your strengths and weaknesses lie.

Verbal communication

In the context of this book, verbal communication is the act of communicating orally with words to one or more people. It can take place face to face, over the phone, via Zoom or FaceTime, from a public stage or through a learning aid like a video tutorial or lecture. It can be informal, for example chatting with friends and family, or more formal such as a business meeting or the Queen's Christmas speech. In most instances (the Queen's speech aside), verbal communication will be part of a conversation, which involves two or more people conversing orally (with words, guys, not kisses) while listening to each other. This will come naturally to many people, especially in a casual situation such as chatting with a mate on the phone or telling your partner what to pick up from the grocery store. The more familiar you are with the other person or people, the easier the conversation flows. There will also be moments with certain people where the conversation is so rigid and stagnant that you question your own sparkle. I think some people are naturally better verbal communicators than others, but I do also think that no matter how good a communicator you are, sometimes the conversational chemistry is just off.

Then, of course, we have the more crucial conversations; the kind of conversations that require thought and emotional intelligence, such as talking to a loved one about what you need from a relationship or articulating your feelings when in the midst of confrontation. Perhaps it's a high-stakes conversation, such as asking your boss for a promotion or pitching a business plan, and it requires planning and emotional restraint. When the stakes of conversing are upped, the pressure can be enough to render a Chatty Cathy mute. I find that self-awareness and clarity around what your message is, which might require a bit of planning, is the best way to navigate these crucial communications.

Non-verbal communication

My sister and I have mastered the resting bitch face. Since we have different mothers, the only logical conclusion is that we inherited it from our father. The problem with the resting bitch face is that most of the time we're just deep in thought, not plotting someone's demise, but it gets misinterpreted because people draw their own conclusions. You see, words are so important when it comes to any kind of communication, but what isn't said can be even more telling. Body language, eye contact, facial expressions, posture and touch are forms of non-verbal communication. They can say so much on their own, but when matched with verbal communication, these non-verbal cues become so powerful. In conversations, I tend to pick up on other people's non-verbal cues more than what they're saying, so I'm particularly conscious of what my body is inferring alongside my words. I hold eye contact with someone to communicate that I'm interested. I resist fidgeting with my hands and stand tall to let them know I'm confident. I'll place my hand lightly on someone's arm and nod in agreement to indicate compassion and understanding, and I ensure my body is always turned towards the person who I'm talking to so they know that I'm present and interested in what they're saying.

Non-verbal communication also includes:

★ Physical appearance. What you're wearing, if you've brushed your hair and if you've recently showered will all contribute to how you're received by others. If you wore jeans and a sweatshirt to a corporate interview, what would that be communicating about you to your potential employer? If you rocked up to a date with greasy hair and dirt under your fingernails, what message would that be sending to your date?

★ Tone of voice. This is so important. You can say the same collection of words a multitude of ways and just change your tone of voice each time, and the meaning of it will completely alter. This is why written communication (see below) can often be misinterpreted, because it's missing tone altogether.

★ Proxemics. This is the physical distance between communicators. Where you stand in relation to the person you're talking to can say so much. It can display intimacy, even when nothing is being said.

I believe that non-verbal communication is something we can all do with strengthening. As someone who was born a good verbal communicator, non-verbal communication was something I had to teach myself and I'm still always conscious of it.

Written communication

As I'm a writer, I love written communication! But even if you haven't made a career out of it, if you struggle to articulate your words verbally in the moment, written communication gives you an opportunity to sort through the jumble in your head and communicate exactly what you want to say. However, that's not always the case. How many times have you read something and thought, 'What are they trying to say? I'm so confused.' The key to good written communication is clarity and being as concise as possible. Whether it's an email, text, cover letter or Facebook post, getting to the point and ensuring that your intention is conveyed is key to successful written communication. Another important thing to remember is that, unlike verbal communication that disappears into the ether once it's spoken, written communication lives on, perhaps in perpetuity.

I've worked with many writers throughout my career, and I can tell you now that just because someone is an epic written communicator, it doesn't mean they're a good verbal communicator. So if written communication is your strength, work it, baby. When I was younger and struggled to articulate how I was feeling verbally, I'd always write it down in a letter so that I was able to explain myself as best as I could to a lover or a friend. If verbal presentations are not your jam at work, then consider putting together a written report for your colleagues. If written communication isn't a strength of yours, know that it can always be taught. Here are my key pointers:

★ Work out what your intention is before you start writing.
★ Determine what the message is you want to convey.
★ Ask yourself, 'Have I said this in a clear way? Could this be misinterpreted?'
★ Do a spell check ALWAYS!
★ Read it out loud to ensure the tone is correct. Sometimes when we hear ourselves say what we've written, we realise that it lacks compassion or whatever emotion needs to be conveyed.

Listening

Unfortunately, listening doesn't always make it onto the list of types of communication, which is crazy, don't you think? Active listening is one of the most important parts of communication, because if we can't listen to the person sitting across from us, we can't effectively engage with them. If you're one of those people who tunes out while the other person is talking and bides time until you get to talk again, you're failing as an effective communicator. Active listening is about being present and observing everything that's happening around you. Used in conversation, it's the process of taking in, remembering and responding to what's being said. It also goes beyond what's being communicated verbally and is about observing their non-verbal cues as well. It's about noticing what's being said, but also what's not being said, and then using that information to connect with the other person in a way where everyone feels heard and acknowledged.

Visual communication

A picture says a thousand words, and we're a visual society. Whether it's a photograph on Instagram, a beautiful piece of art or an image used in advertising to sell a product, the messages that we can convey through a visual medium are endless. Think about children's picture books. With no words, a whole story can be expressed simply through imagery. We do a similar thing through our social media feeds. Your profile is curated to share the story that you want to convey to your followers. While visual communication is often not enough on its own, it's good to be aware that an image is subjective and can be open to individual interpretation, which perhaps is your intention, but if it's not, it's worth understanding how your image could potentially be received.

Energetic communication

I used to work for a guy who I just really didn't like. Not because he was cruel or creepy, but just because something felt energetically invasive about him. I always acted professionally around him. I communicated effectively, I smiled, I did what I was told and, to someone who perhaps wasn't as in tune with energy as he was, I would've gotten away with it. But he could see right through me. He pulled me aside one day and said, 'I don't think you know how powerful your energy is. You say one thing, but energetically I feel something completely different from you.' Hmm, he wasn't wrong.

How are you communicating with your energy? I spoke a lot about vibing with someone in *Make It Happen*. You can feel the energetic frequency of other people before any words are uttered, and we would be kidding ourselves if we didn't consider our own energy and the energy of those around us when it comes to effective communication. Our energetic field is heavily influenced by our thoughts and emotions, and even though you can try to hide how you feel and think, energy never lies. Deep down, you always feel the energy of everything that's happening around you, even if you're not consciously aware of it. This is helpful to keep in mind with your own communication. Are you energetically in the right space to be having that particular conversation? Can you process certain emotions and recognise certain thoughts before effective communication can take place?

I mean, none of this should be surprising, especially for a manifestation aficionado such as yourself (if you're yet to read *Make It Happen*, you soon will be). We already know how profound energy is on our manifestations. There has been some powerful research conducted by the HeartMath Institute that shows the heart carries important data that can be detected energetically by others. The heart has been found to produce the strongest electromagnetic field, stronger than the brain. The wave produced by each heartbeat not only carries out information to every cell within the body, but also to the environment and the people surrounding it. This is why emotions are a powerful source of energy in manifestation. When you align your thoughts with an intention and charge it with a feeling, in that moment you're sending a vibrational signal out into the universe to be able to manifest it.

HOW DO YOU COMMUNICATE?

Like most psychological concepts, figuring out communication types is widely discussed across the internet, but I feel like I could make it easier for you. In my personal experience as a passionate communicator, and someone who holds good communication in high regard, I've come across four main types of communicators based on how you process information – i.e. through thoughts, feelings, facts – and I feel like you're likely to resonate with one or perhaps a combination of a few.

1. Analytical: Meet Alana

Alana is an analytical communicator. She's driven by facts and data-driven information. She's unlikely to make a decision unless there are numbers behind it. She likes to get straight to the point, which can come across as cold and uncaring but she prefers objectivity over ambiguity and hyperbole. Alana doesn't like to sugar-coat things and doesn't have time to over-embellish a story for your enjoyment. She's less emotional, which can come across as insensitive, but it does make her capable of making fair and fact-based decisions. This works for Alana in the office because it shows she's dependable and reliable but when it comes to her personal relationships, she can sometimes lack connection.

2. Intuitive: Meet Ian

Ian is an intuitive communicator. He likes to focus on the big picture rather than getting bogged down in the details and data like his mate Alana. Ian gets frustrated with step-by-step processes and just wants to get to the end goal. He feels into what's needed rather than looking at past results or future projections. He's expressive and engaging, which allows him to create an emotional connection with his audience. Ian is very imaginative and doesn't always let the truth get in the way of a good story. Unfortunately, this sometimes means that his message or intention gets lost in ambiguity. However, he's fabulous at reading the room, which quietly I believe is one of the most valuable assets in communication.

3. Practical: Meet Peter

Peter is a practical communicator and is not too dissimilar to Alana. He thrives on details, lists and instructions but, unlike Alana who can get lost in analysing the data, Peter is more practical and prefers to see tangible results, which means he gets in there and makes it happen. He prefers not to make emotion-based decisions unless it offers relatability and relevance to his argument. Peter lives in the present moment and likes to plan for the future but if you ask him to consider a fabricated scenario to prove your point, he'll struggle to find the relevance. He's all about reality and logical thinking, so ask him questions to get to know him better but expect practical answers. Peter likes confirmation that everything has been understood and he'll let you know if things are unclear.

4. Amiable: Meet Amy

Amy is an amiable communicator who's all about personal connection. She's perceptive, self-aware, emotionally intelligent and makes an incredible listener, which means she's pretty wonderful at creating strong relationships (I mean, she sounds like a catch). She finds a solid balance between practicality and emotion, which makes her flexible and empathetic to others' needs. Amy is very easy to talk to but Alana and Peter might find her a little frustrating as she leads with feeling-based connection.

So we all want to be Amy, or we at least want to have a best friend like Amy, but the truth is, there are strengths and weaknesses to all four of your new mates. Alana and Peter are the kind of communicators that thrive in the boardroom or when you need to make big financial decisions but they're probably less helpful and a little frustrating in relationships when sensitivity and emotional connection are required. Ian and Amy are wonderful when conversing with loved ones or over subjects that require sensitivity and compassion but their emotional capacity might have less of a place in certain work situations or when talking to the tax man, ya know? I personally believe you're more naturally inclined to one of these four types but that's not to say that you can't incorporate little bits of each into your own superhuman hybrid communicator type! That's what's so exciting about self-awareness. Once you can see yourself for who you are, you have the power to adorn and embellish yourself however you see fit.

These are all just observations at this point but it's interesting to know where your natural communication tendencies lie.

COMMUNICATION STYLES

Why does communication seem to feel effortless at times and fail miserably at others? When communication breaks down, it's often because the patterns and habits of how we communicate – aka our communication styles – get in the way. It doesn't matter what type of communicator you are – Alana, Ian, Peter or Amy – style is more related to how you express yourself when communicating.

Have you ever had an encounter with passive aggression? Gosh, it's infuriating. The reason I bring it up is not to get us collectively worked up about passive aggression but to point out that a passive-aggressive person is rarely executing their behaviour with conscious intention. If we look at the four styles of communicating that are often discussed, I think you'll find that you likely swing between all four, depending on the situation and person/people you're conversing with. For me, it's been so helpful to be aware of all four styles because I'll often catch myself in the moment and think, 'Oh God, I think I need to switch styles here if this conversation is going to go anywhere,' and it's likely because of my own ineffective communication.

Passive communication

A passive communicator has difficulty expressing themselves and will likely admit defeat if they feel like their opinion is not being heard or understood. They fail to express thoughts and emotions effectively, which can lead to miscommunication and often resentment. You might communicate like this when you feel intimidated or out of your depth.

The traits of a passive communicator are:
- ★ Lack of eye contact.
- ★ Difficulty saying no.
- ★ A follow-the-crowd type of attitude.
- ★ Poor posture.
- ★ Fidgety.
- ★ Inability to speak up or defend themselves.

They might say stuff like:
- ★ 'That's okay, it's not important.'
- ★ 'I'll just go along with what everyone else wants to do.'
- ★ 'I don't mind what we do.'

Aggressive communication

Aggressive communicators are the opposite of passive communicators. They tend to dominate the conversation, failing to listen to others and talking over the top of them in order to get their point across. They put themselves at the forefront of the discussion and can forget that communication is not a one-way street. You might communicate like this when you're all fired up and you're desperate to be heard.

The traits of an aggressive communicator are:
- ★ Intimidates or threatens others.
- ★ Talks over the top of other people.
- ★ Interrupts frequently.
- ★ Fails to listen.
- ★ Has closed-off body language.

They might say stuff like:
- ★ 'I'm right, and you're wrong.'
- ★ 'There's only one way to do this.'
- ★ 'Because I said so.' (Also, quietly, great Diane Keaton and Mandy Moore movie.)

Passive-aggressive communication

The worst! I'm sorry but there are no redeeming qualities to passive aggression.

Passive-aggressive communication appears passive on the surface but underneath there's resentment that comes through in subtle and indirect ways. You might communicate like this when you're not willing to say what you really mean and you fail to express yourself authentically.

The traits of a passive-aggressive communicator are:
- ★ Frequent sarcasm.
- ★ Their words don't align with their actions.
- ★ Their facial expressions don't match their words.
- ★ They find it difficult to acknowledge emotions.
- ★ They're dismissive.

They might say stuff like:
- ★ 'Fine, whatever.'
- ★ 'I was only joking,' after they've said something rude or critical.
- ★ 'I'm not mad,' when they're clearly furious.
- ★ 'Why are you getting so upset?' OMG, so patronising!

Passive aggression stems from one's own insecurities that are then projected onto the other person. If you find yourself doing this, please get curious about why you're communicating this way. It's the most ineffective form of communication.

Assertive communication

This style is a lesson in effective communication and if you're interested in healthy and helpful communication, aim for this style. Assertive communication encourages open and honest dialogue while still considering the needs of others. When in conversation, an assertive communicator can articulate how they're feeling and take responsibility for their own feelings. You might communicate like this when you have self-awareness and know the advantages of clear and conscious communication.

The traits of an assertive communicator are:
- ★ Able to express desires and needs with confidence.
- ★ Excellent at listening and giving both sides an opportunity to speak.
- ★ Able to say no with conviction.
- ★ Maintains good eye contact.

They might say stuff like:
- ★ 'I respect the needs and opinions of others.'
- ★ 'Is there anything that you'd like to contribute?'
- ★ 'I feel like this. How do you feel?'
- ★ 'No, thank you.' (Remember, you learned about how powerful this phrase is in Chapter 5.)

Exercise 23

WHAT'S YOUR STYLE?

It's likely that you switch between different styles of communication depending on the situation, but if you recognise any of those phrases as something that you've said or might say, take this opportunity to reflect and make any notes in your self-awareness journal about whether or not you have a tendency to be passive, aggressive, passive aggressive or assertive when communicating.

Here's the thing with communication … it's not as easy as just saying what you mean. Often what we think and feel isn't always what's accurately communicated when we attempt to share it, and we also don't always receive the intended message and can be confused by people's intentions. When we can learn how to communicate more effectively, especially with verbal communication, there's less room for the error of miscommunication. But when it comes to written communication, which is devoid of tone and sometimes even context, it can be a lot trickier.

The case of the misinterpreted email

Jordanna,
I've been trying to get hold of you to no avail. It's not okay to leave the office without notice. I've organised a meeting with HR and myself for tomorrow morning in regards to this morning's incident.

Your attendance is imperative. Please don't attend tomorrow
morning's WIP.
Heather*.

Oh, man! I'm getting fired. I'd already forwarded the email to my boyfriend, mum, best friend, her boyfriend and my work wife. 'I'm getting fired, aren't I? This is so faaaaarked!' The consensus was unanimous. I was indeed about to be unemployed.

Let's begin with some context ... Heather was my general manager in a job I worked at when my career in magazines was just kicking off. I'd risen up pretty quickly in an industry that likes to keep you small for as long as possible, and there were a few senior staff members who weren't so keen that I hadn't 'earned my stripes' in the same way they'd been made to.

The incident Heather is referring to was an extremely inappropriate and wildly uncharacteristic (for me) feud that broke out that morning with my editor and I over a design layout. I was a junior writer and my editor really disliked me in such an obvious way that other people in the office felt uber uncomfortable every time she spoke to me. Even at the age of 22, I had the foresight to realise that her behaviour had nothing to do with me. Nonetheless, when a 61-year-old senior member of staff has a go at you, the common reaction is to cop it! Usually, I would have. I'd been copping it for the previous six months but that morning I had a short fuse. I hadn't had a chance to pick up my morning coffee after my bus was running late and I was a little hungover from the night before after drowning my sorrows from another shitty workday.

One of the designers had asked our opinion on a layout for a story neither my editor nor I had worked on and we had very differing opinions about the typeset. Instead of keeping my mouth shut, as I probably should have as a junior member of staff, I instead let her know that I didn't appreciate her constant refusal to agree with anything I said out of pure stubbornness. I believe my words were, 'You're such a bloody stubborn cow.' CRINGE! (She was in fact a Taurean, which would make her a stubborn bull, not a cow.) The bustling office fell silent. I was mortified and as a stumbling apology attempted to fall from my mouth, she gave me this evil smirk as if to say, 'Got ya, bitch!' I slunk into a bathroom cubicle and spent the next hour sobbing there while my boyfriend at the time tried to convince me via text to put my big-girl pants on and get back to work. I didn't. Instead, I made my way to a cinema in Sydney's CBD to catch the 10am screening of *The Devil Wears Prada*. Felt fitting.

When I turned my phone back on after the film had finished, there was a barrage of text messages, voicemails and the afore-mentioned email. The text messages ranged from concerned co-workers to a stern GM. My mother had sent me a 'call me now' text after my snitch of a boyfriend had contacted her, requesting she talk some sense into me, and said snitch had sent me several messages ranging from jovial teasing to 'Jord, do I need to come get you?' I couldn't bring myself to listen to the voicemail that had come from a CBD landline number. I knew it was Heather and I couldn't bear to hear the disappointment in her voice. Then, I opened *the* email. I'm fucked!

After going over it several times with my team of advisors, the general consensus was that I was indeed fucked and it was time to start looking for work. So, that's what I did. I thought that if I could go into the meeting tomorrow with at least an afternoon's worth of job searching under my belt, it might not feel as devastating to hear, 'Bitch, you're fired.' I followed up a lead I had with a friend's start-up that was looking for a copywriter. The position was mine if I wanted it. I start Monday. Sweet! Now I could go into that meeting with some 22-year-old swagger in my step. (Again, CRINGE!)

I rehearsed my apology speech and the acceptance of my career demise several times throughout the sleepless night before that meeting. 'You've got this,' I told myself as I walked into HR's office with my head held high and my shoulders slumped low (because, about to get fired). 'Jordanna, take a seat,' Julie* from HR instructed. I sat opposite her and Heather, unable to look her in the eyes. 'Heather has told me an account of what happened yesterday morning but I'd like to hear it from you.' I tried to make my case but I also knew that I'd acted inappropriately and I deserved what was coming. 'After speaking with a number of staff who were present and who have witnessed your working relationship with Stubborn Cow (she used her actual name, obviously), we've decided to give Stubborn Cow a warning and to move you to another magazine. The role is a little more senior but we think you're up for the challenge.' Heather chimed in, 'I'm sorry you were put in that position yesterday. I've been watching the interaction between you and Stubborn Cow for some time now, and I should have stepped in earlier. You'd just been handling yourself so well that I didn't feel like I needed to intervene but now I can see that I should've.'

Umm, sorry what?! But I've already typed up my resignation letter and been hired at a hipster start-up that pays less and has zero sick pay or annual leave. I spent an entire sleepless night rehearsing how to take this news with grace and strength without bursting into tears or snapping like I did the day before. I mean, I didn't make this up! Heather's email clearly said I was getting fired, didn't it? Let's read it again, knowing that I'm not about to get fired and, in fact, I'm about to get promoted.

> Jordanna,
> I've been trying to get hold of you to no avail. It's not okay to leave the office without notice. I've organised a meeting with HR and myself for tomorrow morning in regards to this morning's incident. Your attendance is imperative. Please don't attend tomorrow morning's WIP.
> Heather.

A dissection

Jordanna, that's my name, so nothing to misinterpret here.

I've been trying to get hold of you to no avail. This is what we like to call a fact. She'd indeed been trying to call me and I was in a cinema with my phone off watching Meryl Streep absolutely nail Miranda Priestly – a more stylish version of the Stubborn Cow this tale revolves around.

It's not okay to leave the office without notice. Also a fact. I didn't even leave a note or send an email to let someone know. And still no indication of being fired just yet.

I've organised a meeting with HR and myself for tomorrow morning in regards to this morning's incident. In my head, the incident was me yelling at my boss and crying in a bathroom cubicle for an hour before skipping work and eating an extra-large popcorn and Sprite at 10am on a Thursday. In actual fact, the incident that Heather was referring to was the insistent workplace bullying that'd been taking place for six months that she hadn't put an end to yet.

Your attendance is imperative. The meeting was about me, so it was imperative that I attend AND they were promoting me to a magazine on a different floor, also imperative that I know that.

Please don't attend tomorrow morning's WIP. Well, yeah, I didn't need to be at a WIP for a magazine I was no longer working for, right?

Heather. That's her name. I'll never forget it.

This email from the spring of 2006 may seem like a simple misunderstanding but it's shaped pretty much all digital communication I've had with employees, employers, clients and the mothers of ex-boyfriends going forward. It's also always on my mind when I receive emails from my publisher or editor asking for edits to a manuscript that make me feel like they hate me, hate my writing and are hell-bent on ways to get out of the contract I signed. People are busy and they don't always have the time to make sure that you're not taking offence or misinterpreting their tone. They have a message to deliver and they assume you're going to receive it as they intended. I'm sure the majority of you could say the same for a text that got misconstrued or an Instagram DM, Facebook or WhatsApp message that got you offside.

So, how can you avoid a similar miscommunication without writing a resignation letter to your boss who's about to promote you? I feel like this is most likely an instance where you've already learned this for yourself. But a handy trick I now do before sending an email or text that has the potential to be received negatively is to read it out loud. Simply taking the words off the screen and reading them through the spoken voice can give a nuance that was never your intention. When it comes to your interpretation of the digital communication you receive, I always check back in for clarity rather than getting on the defence. Truth be told, I get on the defence a lot, so let me reword that by saying I TRY to ask for clarification BEFORE I hop on the defence #onlyhuman. The beauty of written communication is that we have the ability to sit with it, edit it, contemplate its tone and then decide not to send it if we so desire. We don't get this luxury with regular conversation. Make use of this gift!

MANIFESTATION REMINDER

Whether they're being spoken, written or read, words hold their own vibrational frequency. This is why clear and conscious communication is so important – everything you say is contributing to your manifestations. Speak with intention and authenticity and have the types of conversations that will lead you towards a future you desire.

GOOD COMMUNICATION

We've covered the precarious nature of miscommunication (i.e. my email from Heather), and although that was an example of misinterpreting written communication, I reckon most of you can agree that verbal communication has just as much room for error if we're not communicating effectively. Before we dive into some other ways you can become a rockstar communicator, let's get curious about what you feel your strengths and weaknesses are when it comes to communication.

Exercise 24

STRENGTHS AND WEAKNESSES IN COMMUNICATION

Divide a page in your self-awareness journal down the middle. On one side, write 'strengths' and on the other side, write 'weaknesses'. Below are some prompt questions to help you out. Remember, there's nothing wrong with putting something in the weaknesses column. The minute you become aware of it and consider how you might approach it differently when next faced with a situation that allows you to do so, it becomes a strength.

Prompt questions:

(Do I speak too fast or too slow?

(Can I explain things clearly?

(Am I practical in the way I communicate?

(Am I a good listener?

(Do I struggle to say what I mean?

(Do I feel understood?

(Do I use my hands a lot when I talk?

(Am I conscious of my facial expressions?

(Do I speak without thinking?

(Do I find it difficult to speak up?

(Do I get emotional when I'm talking about things that I'm passionate about?

Again, these are all just things to be aware of. No judgement is necessary. There's always room to improve communication, but only once you can accept where your weaknesses are.

Listening (part two)

As we've discovered several times already while learning about the different types of communication and communicators, the most underrated quality of being a good communicator is being able to listen. For a chatty Gemini like me, that meant learning what a gift it was in effective communication to embrace silence.

I had a teacher once whose gift was silence. You would ask him a question, all young and eager, and he would look you dead in the eye and say nothing for what felt like an eternity, but really was just long enough for you to come up with the answer yourself. It's a similar technique used in psychology and counselling. The silence gives you space to contemplate their response and in doing so, you come up with your own. It's really quite brilliant. If we take Mr Martin*'s gift a little further, though, it's in those silent moments where people can feel truly heard. If you're tuning out and just waiting until you can say your piece, you might as well be chatting with your own reflection in the mirror.

Let's take a look at how you can be a better listener:

1. **Be present.** This means that your attention, your thoughts and even your body position are all geared towards the person you're talking to. Listening is so much more than just hearing what someone has to say. It's about understanding what they're saying. When you're rehearsing what you're going to say next in your head while the other person is still talking, you're not being present.

2. **Put down your phone.** Or any other distraction, for that matter. When you're in conversation with someone, your full attention should be on them. Look the person in the eyes and be focused on what they're saying.

3. **Be curious and ask for clarification.** If you're listening and haven't fully comprehended what is being said, ask follow-up questions.

4. **Be aware of your non-verbal communication.** When we're listening for long periods of time, our body language

and facial expressions can start to shift without us being conscious of it. Be aware of this. Part of listening effectively is making the other person feel comfortable and heard. If your face screams 'this is so fucking boring', you may as well have screamed it out loud. Ya feel me?

5. **Be open-minded.** Part of the reason we listen is to learn new things and hear different perspectives and opinions. Allowing people to finish what they have to say before jumping in allows both sides to be heard. And you never know, you might just learn something new.

Authenticity

It may seem pretty self-explanatory but effective communication is about being real and honest about what you think and how you feel. If you're holding back by not being your authentic self and misleading people about who you are, what you stand for, what you believe in or how you really feel, then you're not giving the conversation a chance to evolve authentically in a way that serves you or them. Make sense?

Ask questions

We covered asking follow-up questions when we spoke about listening but I think it's worth mentioning it again. Questions aren't just good for clarification, they also keep the conversation rolling, show that you're interested in what the person is saying, and a good question will require more than just a yes or no response.

Be clear and concise

This is something that I've worked on mastering over the years as a journalist. Quit waffling, folks! Whether it's in conversation or written communication such as an email or text, just get straight to the point. Sometimes, we just keep speaking to fill in gaps in conversation, but once you've made your point and said your piece, do as Mr Martin does and be silent.

Sync verbal communication with non-verbal communication

When I was a teenager, I'd often tune out while my parents were talking to me (I mean, what self-respecting teenager doesn't?). But unfortunately for me, it was written all over my face. Did you know that when your eyes glaze over, it's a visual tell-tale sign? I didn't. I thought it just looked like I was staring at my parents intently but it turns out it looks like you're disinterested and falling asleep. I was also a big eye roller, arm crosser and fidgeter. We still do all of that as self-respecting adults. Telling someone you care about what they're saying while you roll your eyes and sit slumped in your chair sends mixed messages. It's important to be conscious of the fact that what people hear you say and what people see you do will get interpreted simultaneously so it all counts towards good communication.

Read the room by observing others

This is an incredible skill to have. Intuitive communicators are naturally adept at observing, being conscious of and energetically analysing how everyone in the room is feeling, or at the very least what's appropriate behaviour in their presence. For example, if you were a male stand-up comedian and you saw a sea of women in the audience, it wouldn't be the best time to pull out a misogynistic quip (I mean, is there ever a good time?). Or, if you'd arrived to meet a friend excited to share news of your new job promotion but she looked sad and distracted, it would be good to enquire about her state before jumping in to share your good news.

Here are some tips for reading the room.

DO:

★ Observe. The best way to read a room is to play close attention to other people, and not just what they're saying. Look at their non-verbal cues too. It's incredible how much you can tell about how someone is feeling based on their body language, facial expressions and posture.

★ Control how much you talk. If you notice eyes glazing over (I shared the tell-tale signs with you before), it might be time to wrap things up. If you're in conversation, make sure you take frequent pauses so that other people have time to chime in and say their bit.

DON'T:

★ Ignore signals and micro expressions such as frowns, fleeting smiles and raised eyebrows. You don't have to stop what you're saying immediately but use them as an indicator of how people are feeling.

★ Make it all about you. Choosing to ignore what you've picked up on in the room and continue on with what you're saying is making the lines of communication all about you. Don't do that! Not cool.

Have empathy without getting emotionally involved

A huge part of reading the room is about having empathy. Healthy communication is when you're able to step into the person's shoes to understand them better but without allowing yourself to become emotionally involved to the point where their emotions become yours (refer to Chapter 4: Emotions). A good communicator will be self-aware enough to know the difference.

Show understanding

There are so many non-verbal cues you can use to show that you understand what someone is saying. Nodding your head, smiling in recognition, a light touch of someone's hand or shoulder, maintaining eye contact, the list goes on. It may even be appropriate to contribute the odd 'yes', 'aha' or 'I see' to indicate that you're following and interested in what they're saying. If you're reading this and thinking, 'OMG, this is so basic. Who does this woman think she is?', you'd be surprised at how many people don't exercise the courtesy of indicating to the person they're conversing with that they're engaged in the conversation.

If you're nervous, slow down

When we get nervous, we tend to start talking really fast. If this is you and you find yourself stumbling on your words, take a breath and slow the F down. When you speak too fast, you lose the engagement of your audience and you lose track of what you're trying to say. To be clear with your communication, slow down the pace, pause and remember to breathe.

Respect

Lastly, respect is so important in any kind of communication. Sometimes, you may disagree with what the other person is saying, and while you have a right to your opinion, you should never interrupt someone talking or raise your voice to object. If you keep your tone pleasant and respect the other person, it'll be received more openly than if you interrupt, raise your voice or talk over them. Pretty basic manners stuff, right?

Exercise 25

HOW YOU COMMUNICATE

Taking everything you've learned about communication in this chapter, write one paragraph about how you communicate in your self-awareness journal. It can include your strengths and weaknesses, as long as your weaknesses don't become an excuse.

For example, my paragraph would be:

I'm a strong verbal communicator who also enjoys written communication. I have to be conscious at times of my non-verbal cues, as I have a tendency to show how I'm feeling through my facial expressions and body language. I'm a great listener and feel that I'm quite skilled at reading the room and making people feel heard and understood when in conversation with me. I've done a lot of work around being an assertive communicator, but I need to watch that I don't get too passive around people who intimidate me.

LEARNING

I was very average at school and struggled through my higher education. Not because I wasn't intelligent or academic but because I didn't absorb information in the way that school delivered it to me. I found myself having to work overtime to learn things before exams and assessments in a way that I understood. Now don't laugh, but a good chunk of my Year Eight science knowledge was broken down into easy-to-remember raps. My history notes were visual re-enactments in my mind of my friends acting out the roles of women in Ancient Egypt. And before exams, I'd wake up at 3am that morning and cram, because I knew it was my best chance of passing when the knowledge was fresh in my mind.

You see, we all learn and absorb information differently. Unfortunately, most education systems don't take into account that just as students come in many different sizes, are from different cultures and have different family environments, they also learn in differing ways. I could write an entire chapter on the different learning styles but for the sake of this book, I just want to highlight that perhaps you've struggled not just as a student but even at work, simply because you absorb information differently to others. If you do have a massive 'aha' moment as you become more self-aware, I encourage you to look into what you learn about yourself a little bit deeper. As with most things you've been learning about yourself thus far, it's likely you'll identify with more than one style of learning.

Different learning styles:

1. Verbal – learns best through speech and writing.
2. Aural – learns best using sound, music and listening.
3. Kinesthetic – learns best using a hands-on approach.
4. Visual – learns best using pictures and images.
5. Logical – learns best through reasoning and making sense.
6. Solitary – learns best through self-paced studying.
7. Social – learns best in groups.

Exercise 26

WHAT TYPE OF LEARNER ARE YOU?

Grab your self-awareness journal and jot down what your strengths and weaknesses are when it comes to learning and absorbing information. Then, list which learning styles you think sound most like you. Remember, it's likely that you identify with a few different learning styles. In fact, I guarantee they'll overlap.

COMMUNICATION AND THE THREE STEPS OF SELF-AWARENESS

This was an information-heavy chapter and if you're not a verbal learner, then it may have been a little overwhelming for you. But the pay-off is self-awareness and, well friends, you just can't put a price on the value of that! Hopefully you understand yourself a lot better and will be conscious of how you communicate by playing to your strengths and making allowances for your weaknesses.

Step 1: Curiosity

You did several exercises to get curious about your communicative self. If you skipped past the exercises, it's imperative that you go back and do them. Communication is such a huge part of how you interact with the world and if you've struggled with it in the past, perhaps now you have all the information you need to try things differently. If you're looking for some extracurricular lines of enquiry around your communicative self, you might like to look into the following:

★ Is your communication consistent? What are the variables that determine whether you communicate well or not?

★ What do you require to feel more comfortable with communication? This could be adequate preparation, being in front of someone rather than over the phone or even a certain talisman. A friend of mine holds a small tumblestone crystal in her hand when she needs to have an important conversation, as it gives her a sense of safety.

Step 2: Acceptance

If you arrived at this chapter thinking you were terrible at communicating, I hope that you've figured out a few things about yourself and you can now see that everyone has the ability to effectively communicate when they know where their strengths lie. Just like everything in self-awareness, acceptance is integral. It allows you to recognise and accept your weaknesses, and instead of using them as an excuse, you can play to the parts of communication that you're good at. If you can't accept these aspects of yourself and instead make excuses such as, 'I'm not a good communicator,' 'Why don't people listen when I speak?' or 'Why does no one understand me?' then there's no room for improvement or for you to find alternative solutions.

I think the passive-aggressive communication style is a really good example. As much as I harped on about hating passive-aggressive communication, I can choose that tactic when I've got my bitchy pants on. And you know what, friends? It's so not cool. I've had to accept this about myself so I can choose the much more effective alternative of assertive communication. The same could be said for accepting that your non-verbal communication needs some fine-tuning or that the reason people are offended by your emails is because you leave them open to misinterpretation by not being clear.

Step 3: Embodiment

Someone who's able to truly embody what it means to be an effective communicator will have the following traits:

★ Patient listener.

★ Clear and concise in their delivery.

★ Empathetic, but not at the expense of their own emotions.

★ Observant.

★ Clear on their intention.

★ Polite.

★ Respectful.

★ Emotionally intelligent (see Chapter 4).

★ Self-aware (see entire book).

Embodiment is also about being conscious that communication isn't a one-way street and that the other person/people you're conversing with may communicate differently to you. I try to take that into consideration but I also think that if you give the respect to others that you wish to receive, it's generally a good rule of thumb. For example, before I send an email, I read it to myself out loud and ask myself if this is how I'd want to receive this message. Most of the time, I go back in and make it a little more friendly and polite. It's not that my emails are ever rude but sometimes I just get straight to the point without adding flourishes and niceties (yet I like to receive them in return, so I'm getting better at adding them in). If I have to have a serious conversation with a friend about a hard topic, I think about how I'd like to receive the news, and make sure I show compassion and understanding through not just my words but my non-verbal cues too. Knowing all of the rules of effective communication is one thing but just like everything you discover in this book, embodying the teachings is when the real life-changing transformations happen.

CHAPTER 7

Love, Sex & Desire

I've already written a whole book on love, and when I sat down to write this book, I questioned whether it was a necessary inclusion when discussing self-awareness. But there are no ifs or buts about it. Love may be something that you classically experience with a partner but once you have an awareness of how you feel, what you desire, your own pleasure and what you expect from love (not society's expectations), then the whole bloody love, sex, desire game changes! We also all experience, give and receive love differently – to both ourselves and our lovers – so having an awareness of your personal relationship with love enables you to open up to love (and sex) in different ways.

When looking at love, sex and desire as topics of self-awareness, I think the order in which you explore them is of the utmost importance. I'm going to start with desire because even though it wasn't my initial instinct when diving deep into these topics, I realised that desire really does set the foundation for both love and sex. Then, we're going to explore love but more importantly self-love, as it's at the heart of all good love stories. Lastly, we're going to talk about sex (baby), which I'm super stoked about because I know the aforementioned song invites us to talk about it, but nobody ever really does from the perspective of self-awareness.

We're always looking at how to please others or analysing what we don't want. But what about what we do want? We're also going to stick a big fat magnifying glass over societal expectations when it comes to love, sex and desire, and why we're following a rule book nobody actually freaking wrote just because of some whack 'norms' that were created way back when. I am livid that the order I'm rolling content out to you is different to the heading of this chapter but would desire, societal expectations, love, self-love and sex have had the same ring to it? I think not. Reserve your judgements and let's proceed.

DESIRE

I added desire to a chapter about love and sex not because I wanted to discuss it in the vein of sexual desire (although, we will discuss that too) but because desire is something we dismiss without contemplation, forget to make space for and fail to consider when it comes to what propels us forward. You see, our desires give us purpose, drive us towards our intentions and, when it comes to manifestation, give us the fuel required to direct our energy with passion and precision. Our desires lay the foundations for self-love, romantic love, sexual pleasure, our manifestations, goal setting, our successes, what motivates us and living a purpose-driven life. If you can understand the foundational aspects of desire and how it applies in relation to your own self-awareness, you might just gain an insight into love and sex (and all that other juicy stuff I mentioned) that you'd never contemplated before.

What is desire?

This isn't a research tool I use often, but when I was exploring desire for this chapter, I turned to the Bible. Having been raised religion-curious (i.e. 'work it out for yourself, Jord') and attending a Catholic high school, I had this illogical guilt around the concept of desires. I haven't unpacked it completely but, for me, there was a layer of sinful connotation attached to desiring something.

A quick overview of a bestselling book, found in the drawer of all reputable motel chains, says that Christianity views desires as both good and evil. Sin is often committed from the pursuit of destructive desires otherwise known as lusts. These 'lusts' are often shown as cravings for satisfaction of the physical appetites: food, alcohol, sex, money and pleasure (all the good stuff).

Basically, desires are sinful when they fall outside the parameters of Christian morality, and I don't know about you but my desires quite often do. This is not an attack on Christianity, rather an observation of perhaps why I hadn't prioritised my own desires in life. I subconsciously thought that pursuing them was considered naughty.

If we prise desire out of Sunday school's hands and look at it in its simplest form, desire is to strongly wish for or want something (or someone). I have issues with the word wish. I expressed my distaste for it in *Make It Happen:*

> '[Wishing] sets a certain tone of hope and longing for a future that we aren't in control of and for something we believe is out of reach ... even if it's not ... Wishing is something you do on a star. It takes you and your ability to make choices out of the equation. It relinquishes the action piece.'

I believe desire is so much more than strongly wishing for something (sorry, internet dictionary). It's a longing and overwhelming certainty that something, either tangible or envisaged, is meant for you. If we look at it in the context of manifestation, your desires become a road map for your thoughts, feelings, actions and faith to follow. Once you get clear on what you desire for your life, you have a clear, unadulterated path to direct your energy.

Desire and manifestation

All good manifestations start with an intention, and here's a little insider tip for you: your intentions are really just your desires in disguise. We explored setting intentions in depth in *Make It Happen* but if you're not caught up or perhaps you need a little refresher, here's what you need to know about setting intentions.

Intention-setting guidelines

Clarity is your best friend
Developing your self-awareness will help with this. Hopefully by the end of this book you're super clear on what you desire for your present and your future.

Follow the three Ps
Write your intentions in the *present* tense, keep the language around your intention *positive* and keep each intention *potent* (no waffling). The universe hasn't got time for that.

Align your thoughts with your intentions

Our thoughts are incredibly powerful and if you spend your time thinking thoughts that challenge what you desire for yourself, why would they bother manifesting?

Work out how you desire to feel and start feeling those feelings right now

Your feelings create your vibrational frequency. If you can decide how it will feel when your intentions manifest (or when you realise your desires) and start experiencing those feelings now, WOW, the world is your oyster, baby!

Take actions towards your intention

It's all very well to desire a future for yourself, but what responsibility are you going to take to make it happen? Taking actions towards what you desire is a key step in ensuring your intentions manifest.

Have faith that you're worthy and deserving of the things that you desire

It's one thing having a desire, it's quite another to have deep faith that you're worthy of it. When it comes to your intentions, faith teaches us two things: one, that you believe you're worthy of your desires and two, that if your intention doesn't manifest then it's because something better is on the way.

Desire and self-awareness

When we look at desire in the context of self-awareness, there are a few layers to it, but let's start with desire in its most generalised form. First, you need to get curious about what you desire. It might surprise you to know that many people don't even get to this point. Have you taken the time to ask yourself what you desire in life? If not, don't sweat it, kid, as we're going to do all the digging in a moment.

Then, you must accept your desires as a part of who you are. Again, we often fall short at this step by either shunning our desires out of guilt or not believing that we're worthy of them.

Lastly, when you can embody what it means to covet something AND take action to attain it, your desires become not only a recognition of the self being deserving of more of what it already possesses, but also, much like your values, your desires keep you accountable and in alignment with what's most true for you.

Psychotherapist and relationship and sexuality expert Esther Perel has a really beautiful take on desires: 'You can force people to do, [but] you can never force them to desire. [Desire is] the ultimate expression of our free identity.' What a wonderful way to marry desires and self-awareness. If we can dig deep within ourselves and extract exactly what we desire from the depths of our soul, not only do we have access to a full expression of who we are, but also there's a sense of freedom (and power) in recognising that we're only ever bound by the desires we choose for ourselves.

I believe that the best place to start to understand what it is you desire is to first look at what lights you up. When you can connect to the things in your life that make you feel all kinds of wonderful, it's easier to understand what you do and don't desire. Make sense? Let's get curious.

Note: We're going to explore desire in terms of love and sex as we move through this chapter, but if there are things in either of those categories that set you on fire, feel free to throw them into the mix. We're diving deep into your soul, remember, so only *you* get to say what goes!

WHAT LIGHTS YOU UP?

It's a simple question to ask but when it comes to answering it, sometimes the answers don't flow so easily. So let's not overthink it. Grab your self-awareness journal and without giving it too much thought, write down all of the things that light you up.

Note: If you're unsure of what 'lights you up' means, think about what brings you joy, what makes you feel aligned, motivated and inspired, and the things in life that excite you. There are no right or wrong answers here, nothing too big or too small, everything goes.

Societal expectations

Many of our desires aren't our own. The trick is deciphering what we desire for ourselves and what we desire because of societal expectations, peer pressure or parental influence. Being self-aware is evaluating what you actually want and knowing that it doesn't have to fit in with everyone else's standards. I used to live my life in constant pursuit of societal norms. It was subconscious, of course, but I found myself feeling constantly disappointed for failing to achieve what society expected of me.

When the COVID-19 pandemic hit, all of sudden people's timelines – the timelines created by societal constructs – started to feel stunted. The thought of continuing to lose precious time was overwhelming, with no end date in sight. What was going to happen to our plans to travel the world? How were we meant to meet the love of our life if we couldn't leave our own home?

What about the careers we'd worked so hard at, only to be dealt one obstacle after another? During 2020, in the midst of the first year of the pandemic, I began to truly question why I'd spent so much of my time pandering to the expectations of what society deemed an acceptable timeline for my life. Surely it was okay for my own desires to not fit neatly into the same linear process as everyone else's. So I began to pull apart my desires and decide which ones were mine, and which ones belonged to an external standard.

As a teen, I was convinced I'd be married by 25 and have a baby by 27. That was a desire of an 18-year-old terrified of being alone. A teenager who'd witnessed a single mother raise her. A teen obsessed with Hollywood rom-coms and love stories. Now, in my late 30s, I don't prioritise marriage. It doesn't mean anything to me. I desire commitment and security, but marriage doesn't equal either of those things in my eyes. If someone's going to stay or leave, I know for a fact that a marriage certificate isn't the deciding factor. This isn't the result of coming from a broken home or seeing friends get divorced before I've been engaged; it's just the realisation that what I desire is how marriage has been sold to us, but not the reality of what marriage truly is.

I do, however, want to have a baby so desperately but I know that my desire to have a baby comes as a package and that package is a family. A mother and father who not only love that baby unconditionally but who are also in love with each other. This is my strongest desire yet I almost had to let it go this year. In fact, it made me realise that, unlike marriage, the societal construct of family is one that *is* important to me even if I tried to convince myself it wasn't. I did have to seriously question whether I didn't want to raise a baby on my own because I genuinely didn't want to or because societal norms told me it was unacceptable.

You see, I didn't come from a cookie-cutter family. I've grown up with step-parents, half-siblings, several family homes and shared custody, so I get unconventional families. In fact, I embrace them. I watched my mum ace being a single parent and I know I would've aced it too. I would've embraced it wholeheartedly but it took my pregnancy loss to realise that it was okay to mourn the baby I didn't get to ever know and at the same time recognise the prospect of doing it alone was something I'd never desired for myself. Part of recognising and accepting your desires is the awareness that it's okay to want the best for yourself as long as it's coming from inside of you and not external expectations. I also realised that as much as I want a baby, what I want even more is a strong, secure and exceptionally loving relationship. Instead, I have three published books.

That may seem like an unusual parallel and that's because it is. It's fucking ridiculous but people will often use my career achievements as a consolation prize for why I haven't settled down even though my biological clock is ticking at a deafening decibel. Perhaps you do this to yourself too. I certainly did. I convinced myself that I couldn't have all my desires at once. I couldn't have love and a career. I told myself that the only reason these Insta-worthy family units existed was because they hadn't prioritised career goals like I had. Which we all know is bullshit. But whether we want to believe it or not, we still bow to the notion that perhaps women can't have it all or at least I convinced myself of it so I could sleep better at night.

The truth is that I haven't 'settled down' because I haven't met the love of my life. And as hard as that is to admit, it's the truth, and no number of bestselling books will ever make up for that. The one desire that leads me to a string of desires that follow (i.e. babies, beautiful big home, solid family unit, fulfilling love-fuelled life) all rest on that first desire: to fall in love with my person. But as I push 38, feeling robbed of two precious years due to COVID-19, I've had to ask myself if this is a desire I might need to let go of or if this is just society telling me that I've run out of fucking time.

Societal expectations don't just stop with marriage and babies. Here are some more I've wrestled with over the years:

★ **Don't sleep with someone on the first date or they'll think you're easy.** According to who? There are so many rules that were made up by God knows who when it comes to sex. We're going to explore your own sexual desires shortly but I encourage you to start questioning what rules you follow because they're important to you and which ones you follow because some fuddy-duddy made a rule about it way back when.

★ **Pink is for girls and blue is for boys.** Okay, this is a super basic one but it illustrates my point. We have cerebral and emotional connections to certain things without ever questioning why. This colour connotation is really no different to why you believe you should've been married by your early 30s.

★ **Stay youthful and beautiful.** See also, stay skinny but curvy.

★ **Be successful but not more successful than a man.** I fear that all of my examples keep coming back to patriarchal expectations but I'll just leave that here and you can draw the conclusions that you see fit.

The societal expectations that you feel beholden to might differ from mine. They may be around owning a home, travelling the world, reaching a top-tier level in your career or having a certain amount of money in the bank. Self-awareness begs you to look at what you desire in your life and decide whether you can say without a doubt that those desires are yours and yours alone, or if they've been swayed by the expectations so ingrained in us that we never even thought to question them.

MANIFESTATION REMINDER

The universe doesn't abide by societal constructs and expectations. Let timelines go, surrender to your own precious timing and know that the universe favours those who continue to choose faith over fear.

Exercise 29

SOCIETAL EXPECTATIONS

Let's shine a spotlight on the expectations you've placed on yourself simply because of a societal construct or expectation that was created God knows when by God knows who. Grab your self-awareness journal and write down all of the social expectations to which you've subconsciously been conforming.

Here are some questions you can prompt yourself with to see if you've been holding yourself to an external standard:

(Do I ever feel like I'm falling behind in my life compared to my peers?

(Do I put pressure on myself to reach a certain milestone? And if so, who set that milestone?

(Do I have a timeline for what I want to achieve in my life?

(Have my failures in the past been based on my own standards or someone else's?

Self-awareness is constantly questioning why you desire what you do. If social norms and fabricated timelines didn't exist, how much more satisfied would you be with your own life?

LOVE

Writing a book about love was one of the most challenging writing assignments I've ever had. Not because love is a difficult subject to write about or because I'm not teen-girl obsessed with love stories, but because a huge part of writing *Higher Love* was shining a big ol' spotlight on myself and dismantling everything I knew about love so that I could approach it from a self-aware and fully embodied state. Most of us don't do this, FYI. We make love all about the other person. We waste precious time trying to become everything someone else wants us to be by bending, shifting and accommodating their desires at the expense of our own. Most of the time it's subconscious and likely a slow progression but this is why self-awareness should be the starting point for all epic love stories. It surprised many readers of *Higher Love* to learn that to manifest more love in your life, you need to figure out who you are, what lights you up and how you want to feel in love. There's hardly a mention of the other person in the love story. If you're keen to explore love in depth as part of your self-awareness journey, here's an exercise to help you navigate love from a self-aware space.

Exercise 30
HOW DO YOU DESIRE TO FEEL IN LOVE?

I presented this exercise in *Make It Happen* and *Higher Love*, and here it is again because it's so goddamn effective. If there's only one self-awareness exercise you do concerning love, let it be this one.

Grab your self-awareness journal and write a comprehensive list of how you desire to feel in love (or if it's more helpful, in a relationship). Be aware that this isn't a list of how you want them to make you feel, rather the feelings that you desire to have easy access to when in love.

This list works twofold. Firstly, it creates a vibrational frequency around you that will attract a similar frequency towards you (hello, kismet love story). Secondly, the list can then be used as a barometer to help you determine if you're able to access those feelings you desire when you're with them.

After doing much research and writing, I've learned that when it comes to love, I get bored super easily. This isn't something I'm proud of. It's something I've worked at over the years, but knowing this about myself has allowed me to stop fleeing every time I feel boredom creep in. Having this awareness has given me the opportunity to take a breath and question if my sudden new-found boredom is warranted or just a new stage of comfort in the relationship? Having an awareness that in some cases it's me and not them has given the relationship some more room to breathe while I work on my own shit. I've also learned that for me, true attraction stems from intellectual stimulation and a sense of humour. They are non-negotiable. Even if I can connect on every other level with a person, if those two things are missing, then the relationship has no legs.

Here's where things get interesting, though. What I realised after a little self-reflection was that the things I desire and can recognise in myself when it comes to loving others are all things I desire and recognise within myself as an individual. I get bored with myself so easily (not just partners), and I've had to work on ways to be okay with the mundanity and comfort of life without having to constantly be striving, creating and discovering shiny new things. The things that I desire from a partner, such as intellect and humour, are things I admire and desire greatly within myself, and what I'm looking for is a way for those parts of myself to be seen and complemented by another. So it makes sense, then, that to truly show up in love, we have to first look at how we choose to love ourselves.

Love thyself

If you're rolling your eyes because you know self-love is important but you struggle with it, just bring your eyeballs to a halt for a minute while I try and get you back on self-love's side. I've worked with hundreds of women over the years discussing self-love in lots of different ways, and although we all know we're meant to talk to ourselves more nicely, treat ourselves better and love ourselves more, there's still that voice in our head that says we're not worthy, we'll never be enough, we're average, we're ugly, etc. It's not just women, either. Men experience this too. I was flabbergasted (great word, please use it more) at how many men contacted me after reading *Make It Happen* to tell me that the self-love conundrum plagues them too.

My relationship with self-love is always evolving. I've written about it in my previous books and each time I revisit it, I find a new way of tackling it – of making it easier to acquire and more palatable – because as much as we spend our whole lives pursuing love, holding it up to an impossible ideal, getting lost in romantic daydreams and desiring to be loved unconditionally by another, when it comes to loving ourselves, the one thing that we have 100 per cent control of, we choose not to. Pretty crazy (read: stupid), huh? Any kind of love we desire, whether it's from a partner, friend, relative, dog or colleague, is really just a desire of what we want from ourselves. Sit with that for a minute. It makes sense, doesn't it? Think about it … if you could love yourself the way you desire to be loved by someone else, what would that feel like? And more importantly, what would be possible for you?

Everyone wants to feel desirable, but have you ever considered whether you find yourself desirable? Try and banish the immediate association of desires with sex (although if you find yourself sexually desirable, run with it) and think about all of your desirable qualities. I do this often, especially in moments when I'm feeling less than or I've experienced some sort of failure or disappointment. At first it might feel uncomfortable but trust me, this is one of the first steps in learning to love yourself more, and need I remind you what the flow-on effect of that is? LOVE, it's love!

MANIFESTATION REMINDER

Your ability to manifest and your self-worth are directly correlated. In the areas of your life where your self-worth is low, you'll likely struggle to manifest with ease. But in the areas of your life where your level of self-worth is high, you'll find manifestation a breeze. Increasing your level of worth comes down to choosing to love yourself more and assuring yourself that you're worthy of all of the things you desire in your life.

Exercise 31
YOU ARE DESIRABLE!

Grab your self-awareness journal (it's getting a good workout) and at the top of a new page, I want you to write 'I am ...' You're then going to list all of the desirable qualities that you possess.

Here's a snippet of my list:

> *I am ... clever, witty, attractive, sexy, trustworthy, generous, funny, kind, empathetic, compassionate, communicative, forgiving, motivated, courageous, honest and independent.*

If there's a part of you that's freaking out that you're not going to have anything to write, trust me, you will. Also, nobody else is going to read this list, so if you're worried about sounding full of yourself or egotistical, know that recognising what your desirable qualities are is a beautiful and necessary step towards self-love.

I think the biggest misconception about self-love is the notion that it's about an endless stream of positive affirmations, indulgent bubble baths and gratitude journalling. While I'm not here to take any of those things away from you, I don't believe they're the nitty-gritty acts of self-love that'll create a more intimate relationship with yourself. Real self-love is about being brutally honest and asking yourself the difficult questions. It's about accepting who you are and getting curious about your potential. It's about inviting yourself to be challenged and to frolic outside of your comfort zone. It's about being gentle and nurturing like you would with a child. It's about recognising that you are a dichotomy of light and dark.

Self-love is continually asking yourself, 'How can I show up for others in the way I desire without compromising myself?' Self-love is committing to self-awareness (you're winning at this) and staying connected to self, even when you're not all that chuffed about what you see. It's knowing that you always have the choice to take responsibility and turn things around because you value yourself and you're bloody worth it. Last but not least, self-love is choosing to love yourself despite all of the things that make you feel like you can't. Let me explain …

Love yourself despite …

This is a game-changing self-love tool. Once I've explained it to you and you've put it into practice, you're going to find self-love a bazillion times more accessible. Every time I address a room full of people about loving themselves more, I get a barrage of rebuttals about all the things they try to love about themselves but fail to. And I get it. There are certain parts of my body that I really dislike, and no amount of self-massage or positive affirmation is going to change that. But what if I committed to loving myself *despite* the fact that there are parts of my body that aren't ideal to me? Nobody is saying you need to love and embrace all parts of yourself, but you can always choose to love yourself despite the fact that you're not perfect. Of course, this extends further than your physical body. Can you love yourself despite feeling lonely? Can you love yourself despite having eaten all the Tim Tams? Can you love yourself despite not successfully completing a task? Can you love yourself despite failing to adhere to societal expectations? Can you love yourself despite it all? Because *this* is when self-love matters. Self-love is not about loving yourself enough or loving yourself more, it's about loving yourself in the moments when you need love the most.

SEX

I'm about to tell you a personal tale about sex. I think it's an important one, because I don't know about you, but nobody ever taught me how to be self-aware in the bedroom. The focus has always been on the other person, and although I've always been seeking personal pleasure between the sheets, I'm not sure I've ever put my own desires ahead of my lover's. Anyway, pop on the kettle, make yourself a cuppa tea and enjoy this tale of sexual discovery. Afterwards, we'll chat about what I learned so that hopefully you can extract some lessons too.

How do you know if you're good at sex?

Being good at sex and having good sex aren't the same thing. I remember a friend professing to me that she was good at sex. 'If I achieve nothing in my life, write on my tombstone: Lily* was good in bed.' 'But how do you know?' I innocently enquired. 'Is it good because you're enjoying yourself? Is it good when the other person feels satisfied? Is it about mutual satisfaction? Have you been told you're good at sex?'

She looked at me, puzzled, 'Are you *not* good at sex?' I left that encounter befuddled in a Carrie Bradshaw hanging-question kind of way. Can we ever really know if we're good at sex? I've had good sex and I've had bad sex, but mostly I've had pretty average sex. We all have, right? RIGHT?!

I'm not sure you can judge from your own enjoyment if you're good at sex because I've been with plenty of partners who've enjoyed themselves thoroughly while I've faked my way into ecstasy. They would call that good sex. I wouldn't. I've been with partners where our bodies are so in sync I've felt as if I'm the lead in one of those sweaty sexy dance movies yet I haven't reached orgasm. I'd still classify that as good sex whereas others might not. Equally, there have been times where sex is fumbly, mechanical and apologetic, and eventually he reaches some sort of climax and collapses satisfied while I lie there somewhere between mortified and relieved that it's over. Was it my lover's fault? My fault? The combination of our two bodies? In those instances, would Lily be able to make it good because she's good at sex? You see my point, right?

I lost my virginity at age 17 to my first boyfriend. It was slow and sweet but also rigid and kinda painful, and although practice didn't make perfect, it definitely got better over time. With neither of us having any prior sexual experience, we acted out sex the way we imagined it would go, but more realistically what we'd witnessed on screen. While I was inspired by the likes of *Sex and the City* and *Cruel Intentions*, he was inspired by more lowbrow, straight-to-DVD titles (if you catch my drift), with neither adequate teaching aids.

However, in our two-and-a-half years together discovering a sexual relationship for the first time, I learned a lot about what I loved about sex and also what I'd never try again. There was something explorative and risk-free about traversing the sexual landscape of our youth knowing that we were both on equal footing. There were no ex-partners to compare with, consent was always discussed and obtained and sex wasn't used as a weapon or fishing net. It was sweet and exciting, and our time together was one of the more sexually adventurous relationships I've had because everything was a new frontier. After that, sex got bloody complicated.

The guy after him was a total jerk. It was my first experience of being used for sex. At first, I couldn't see what was happening and I was just flattered someone wanted to have sex with me, but slowly I cottoned on to the fact that sex was indeed a tool of manipulation when placed in the wrong hands. In hindsight, this relationship was a defining moment on the gravitas that sex can have on your own insecurities and I'm saddened to say that it set an imprint for most of my 20s. I've spoken to many women about their second sexual partner. I think it's almost more telling than the person that you lost your virginity to. You have some experience under your belt but only with the one person and what you start to realise very fast when your sexual experience increases is that everyone does sex differently.

At the age of 37, I have a friend who's just about to experience a second sexual partner for the first time. I'm not talking about a polyamorous type of situation, I'm talking *ever*. Having married her high-school sweetheart at the age of 23, she's only ever had sex with the one man. As she nears her 40s, recently divorced, she's about to know the excruciatingly nerve-wracking experience of having sex with a new partner for the first time. I've acted all cool and relaxed when she's voiced her concerns – instead making her feel excited to get to play with another man's junk – but the truth is that I still get nervous when I have sex with a new partner for the first time and I'm in way deeper than two dalliances on my tally board.

Would someone who's good at sex get nervous about that shit? I mean, what's there *not* to be nervous about? There's the whole having to be naked in front of someone for the first time, sure, but I'm also nervous about what he looks like naked and what sort of a penis he's going to possess (underwhelming, overwhelming, circumcised, uncircumcised?). Will I react accordingly to whatever is unveiled or will shock and/or disappointment be evident across my face? Will we start traditional and safe or jump straight into his favourite kinks? What if his kinks are too kinky or my moves are not to his taste? What if our bodies don't fit together? What if sex changes everything? I mean that's not really a what if, as sex does change everything! I sincerely hope my friend gets a gentleman/sex God for her second first time.

I'm not going to walk you through every sexual partner I've had, mostly because there's nothing particularly exciting to report. Would there be more to report if I was good at sex? I'm not sure what qualifies as a long list – I don't think mine is excessive – but surely it's long enough to get some kind of an idea as to whether or not I'm 'good at sex', as Lily so eloquently put it. I contemplated calling some ex-partners to enquire about my skills in the bedroom but opted against it. How does one answer that question in earnest? They all seemed to thoroughly enjoy themselves at the time but if you had to critique someone's sexual prowess, surely it would be in relation to other lovers and I wasn't about to subject myself to a ranking system.

Since I wasn't willing to quiz ex-boyfriends about my performance (because, awkward), I decided to ask a bunch of random customers at a small cafe in the seaside town of Byron Bay the same question: 'Are you good at sex?' These were their responses …

Doreen*, 41, bisexual: 'I like to please my partner during sex. It weighs more heavily on my satisfaction than my own personal pleasure. So if he/she is enjoying him/herself, then I'd say I am doing well. So yes, I would say I'm good at sex.'

Gia*, 24, heterosexual: 'I've only been with one guy since we were 18. I don't know what sex is like with other people but I would say I'm good at sex. We both enjoy ourselves … is that good sex?'

I don't know, Gia. That's what I'm trying to figure out …

Joseph*, 36, homosexual: 'Shit, I don't know. I think so. Actually yes, I would say I'm good at sex. I've definitely had bad sex but I'm not sure that was my fault. Well, now you've got me questioning it.'

Sorry, Joseph. I sympathise with your confusion, but if anyone's to blame, I think we can agree that it's Lily.

Tony*, 32, heterosexual: 'Am I good at sex? Absolutely.' 'But how can you be sure?' I prompt. 'Well, she tells me how much she likes it.' Tony starts questioning himself, 'Why ... what did she say?'

I don't know Tony, Tony's girlfriend or any of his ex-lovers. But most of the men and women I spoke to that day (there were 15) all gave me a version of, 'Yeah, I'm good at sex. If they're enjoying themselves, it's good.'

I wasn't buying it because here's the thing ... I've faked more orgasms than I've had actual orgasms during penetrative sex. I've feigned enjoyment in order to make the experience pleasurable for my partner, which quite honestly doesn't make it bad sex in my eyes. But if my partner knew that my moans were slightly exaggerated for his pleasure, would he worry that he wasn't good at sex? Or does it just make me a liar? (Don't answer that!) Pinocchio is well aware of the deceit. *Sigh* Much like Doreen, I too derive satisfaction from my partner's pleasure. But by me not reaching climax, does that make me bad at sex or them bad at sex? And can someone who's good at sex make someone who's not good at sex better?

Many sex experts would tell me that I'm doing myself and my lover a disservice by faking an orgasm, and look, I wouldn't disagree. I've convinced many ex-partners that I liked what they were doing when the truth is I felt nothing. This gave them no room for improvement or a differentiation between what actually felt good and what I indicated felt good. If this is the means by which we judge being good at sex, then maybe I am bad at it ...

I spoke to a girlfriend (not Lily) about the best way to solve this good-at-sex riddle. She suggested I binge-listen to a famous sexpert's podcast to come to a definitive conclusion about how to be better in bed. 'I'm not sure I need to be *better* in bed,' I defensively proclaimed. 'I just want to understand what the determining factors of someone who's good at sex are.' Why was this such a hard question for people to answer? Was I the first person who'd ever questioned this? 'What does it matter, Jord?' she said. 'If you enjoy sex and your partner seemingly enjoys it, isn't that enough?' She was right, it should've been enough but I've had the hankering to be the master at everything I attempt for as long as I can remember so my quest continued.

Note to self: Go and see a therapist about your incessant need to be the best at everything and take a goddamn breath, woman!

So, in the name of research, I spent a weekend bingeing sex podcasts and here's what I learned: sex is subjective AF, which, to be honest, confused me even more. There's no right or wrong way to please someone, as long as they're experiencing something that's pleasurable to them, but should that trump your own experience of pleasure? And if what pleases them doesn't please you, then where are you left? A basic understanding of sexual consent tells us that both parties need to agree to sexual activity and that consent can be retracted at any time. But what about sexual pleasure? If you're feeling nothing and your partner is in a state of ecstasy, it seems pretty selfish to leave them with a 'thanks, but no thanks' simply because your socks are still firmly on your feet.

So then I guess being good at sex comes down to who you're having sex with. Which leads me back to a response from my awkward hour in the Byron Bay coffee shop. Meet Felix*.

Felix, 48, heterosexual: 'Good sex comes down to compatibility. With the right partner, the sex is great. With the wrong partner, it doesn't matter what kinda moves you pull, the sex is always going to be bad. I've found that the right ingredients for good sex are communication, honesty, an open mind and chemistry.'

Felix makes a very good point. In the past, I've admittedly failed on all four fronts, especially when it comes to communication and honesty (à la my fake orgasm confession). I could tell Felix was good at sex. He was by definition sexy but I've had sex with sexy men who were more concerned with flexing for me than pleasuring me. I recall this one poser who'd lie down with his arms bent behind his head like a Calvin Klein model so that his abs would protrude and his biceps could be seen from a more flattering angle. It was his version of sexy but I felt like I was riding a 2D pull-out centrefold. I needed his hands on my hips, my breasts and my thighs, not supporting his over-inflated ego. Felix's sexiness was different. It was attributed to his deep understanding that sex was between the two people (or more, if that's your flavour) taking part, and what makes sex good sex is the connection between the parties involved. If you're good at whatever you and your partner deem to be good – a mutual satisfaction – then that's indeed good sex. But is that also the definition of sexual chemistry?

Sexual chemistry

Sexual chemistry has been something I've searched for in every relationship. It's important to me. To some people it's not as high on their compatibility checklist but, for me, if sexual chemistry and synchronicity are lacking, well then you may as well just be dating a mate. Chemistry is difficult to describe at the best of times, but sexual chemistry is a whole other level because, let's be honest, you can have sexual chemistry with someone and not connect with them in any other way. I dated one guy who I had incredible sexual chemistry with – we couldn't keep our hands off each other. I couldn't stand the guy, though. I've never had so little to talk about with someone in my life, but whenever we took our clothes off, something just took over. The sex was electric, but was it good? Yes! Yes it was! But the fact that I got nothing out of it but good sex kind of diluted the 'good' bit.

As soon as it was over, I went back to being irritated by him. I stayed with him way longer than I should've. Why do we stay when the sex is good but nothing else? Humans seek pleasure, so much so that we can push aside logic and rationale in order to pursue it. But what I came to realise after great sex that was too often unaccompanied by great anything else (is that part of the thrill?) was that what's far more appealing long term is the pleasure of being respected, of sparkling conversation, of quality time and, for me, the feelings of being safe and secure.

What Felix and I both agreed on, after a very sexy discussion about being good at sex at 10am on a Tuesday morning post–long blacks, is that sexual chemistry isn't something that can be rational-ised or cerebrally processed. Sexual chemistry is visceral and often an indescribable physiological reaction but what does give it extra juice is when there's chemistry on all other layers – emotionally, intellectually, spiritually and I'm going to throw in comically for good measure (although Felix didn't find that as important).

'What's the number-one thing you need to feel satisfied when it comes to sex?' Felix turned the tables on me and I suddenly under-stood the sexiness of good communication. I found it hard to come up with only one thing because after my inquisition into good sex began, I'd realised that there was a host of things I required to really enjoy sex. When it came down to it, though, I decided the one factor that allowed me to put on my best performance and also receive sex in the best possible way was if I felt safe.

'Feeling safe and secure?' I replied without conviction, wondering if that made me sound boring and prudish. Of all my ex-lovers, my favourite sexual partner had nothing to do with the sex itself, it was in the moments that followed. The sex was mutually pleasurable (albeit a tad predictable) but he had this extremely masculine and not at all needy way of holding me after the deed was done. It's hard to describe what set it aside from other post-coital embraces, but it's been a high I've chased ever since. It made me feel safe and secure after the silence that engulfs what was merely seconds ago a sweaty, vocal, love-making sesh, and it was clear that it also gave him a sense of belonging and security too. In my eyes, that after-sex hold trumped every other sexual partner I've had.

Those moments after sex are very illuminating to my overall sexual satisfaction. If I've just had amazing sex and then my partner's desire for me disappears post-climax, he goes to do something else, he rolls over and goes to sleep or insert anything other than spending a measly two minutes lying there together, then the entire experience is ruined. Spending time together post-romp makes me feel safe and seen, and it's become a sexual non-negotiable for me.

'Safety is absolutely important. If you feel comfortable and safe, you're better able to explore new sexual terrains. It empowers you and it empowers them. Safety is critical.' It was official: Felix had become my sexual tutor. I made a mental note to ask Felix what he does for a living before our second coffee was complete. 'And then what comes next after safety?' he enquired.

I sat with this for a minute and settled on my top three:

1. **Mutual satisfaction.** It would be inaccurate and dishonest to say that my partner's pleasure isn't paramount to mine because it is. But what's important, and I could do better at communicating, is how I could experience pleasure better. I'm such a great communicator in all other aspects of my life so it's time to bring those skills to the bedroom.

2. **Humility.** Sex can't be taken too seriously, and clearly my recent descent into madness trying to discover the secret recipe to being the best at sex implies that I've been taking sex a little more seriously than necessary. I do enjoy when a sex fumble is met with laughter instead of anxiety and when a not-so-great sex session is met with a 'let's try again' rather than a line in the sand.

3. **Fun.** Binge listening to that sex podcast made me feel like sexual satisfaction was a bloody Holy Grail bestowed upon those worthy to experience sex as a spiritual awakening. While there's absolutely nothing wrong with making sexual pleasure a spiritual experience, it just feels like a lot of fucking pressure, you know?

'You know, you can decide at any moment if that list changes. That's what's so beautiful about sex – it's fluid. If you're with the right person, it grows with you and the relationship. As long as you're clear on your intentions, sex is whatever you and your partner want it to be.' Felix gave me a hug and thanked me for the coffee. 'Call your friend Lily and ask her again why she thinks she's good at sex ...' And then sexy Felix disappeared like an apparition into the bustling Byron breeze.

A waiter came over to collect our empty coffee mugs. 'I saw you talking to Felix,' he began. 'He's so easy to talk to, isn't he? Do you know what he does?' Umm no, waiter, he disappeared before I could ask him. 'He's a neurologist, you know, a brain doctor. He works at one of the universities researching the effect of love on the brain.' Of course he does ... Felix the love doctor, I'll never forget you.

The next day, I called Lily. It'd been three years since our original conversation. A conversation that plagued me during every sexual experience that followed.

Me: 'Hey Lil, remember when we were having wine at your place that time after we'd been out for your birthday lunch and you boasted to me that you were good at sex?'

Lily: 'Nope, don't remember that, how arrogant. Did I really say that?'

Me: 'Um yes, Lily, you did, and you sent me into a three-year spiral trying to decide whether or not I too was good at sex.'

Lily: 'Sorry, you what?' *insert tears of laughter* 'Of course you're good at sex. You've had plenty of good sex – you've told me about it. But really good sex comes down to who you're having sex with, right? You can't be good at sex if you're having sex with someone you have no sexual chemistry with.'

Me: *Hangs up the phone* 'LILY!'

So, here's what I learned during my quest to figure out what makes someone good at sex … First of all, don't listen to drunk girlfriends brag about their sexual escapades. Secondly, sex might be shared with another person, but it's important that you're clear on what your desires and values are, what brings you pleasure and what feelings are important for you to feel during sex. Felix the love doctor also made a couple of great points regarding connecting with a sexual partner: clear communication, honesty, an open mind and, of course, indescribable sexual chemistry. Since my conversation with Lily three years ago and my morning with Felix, I realised that open communication with my partner makes sex a million times better, and although their sexual satisfaction is important to me, I've also realised that my sexual satisfaction should be equally important to me (and them, after all. It takes two to tango).

So, how can you discover it for yourself without having a life crisis at the hands of a friend called Lily? Have lots of sex! Wait, is that good advice? What I mean is that sex is explorative and with each new partner comes new terrain to explore. The only way to have 'good sex' is to be working out what works for you and your partner and what doesn't. Also, be conscious that this might shift over time, which is why communication is so important. I know I've talked about sex in terms of relationships and of course sex absolutely takes place in lots of other different scenarios but if pleasure and satisfaction are your priority, then I actually think most of the above applies to a one-night stand, a fuck-buddy-type situation or any other way that you derive pleasure. *Raises glass* Great sex for everyone!

Exercise 32

LET'S MAKE GOOD SEX GREAT!

It's time to allow yourself the freedom to figure out what you desire from sex instead of mimicking whatever popular culture has told you sex should be. That's the ultimate form of sexual liberation. So, grab your self-awareness journal, because we're about to explore your sexual desires, your sexual limitations (what you do and don't consent to) and how you want to feel during sex. I know, it's a lot, but I guarantee that a bunch of you are sexually active and have never contemplated this stuff. Oh, and if you're reading this and you're in a long-term relationship and think this stuff doesn't apply because you're too far in, think again. There's always time to reinvent your sex life and make it more rewarding for you.

SEXUAL DESIRES

What do I desire for myself sexually? You can be as graphic as you like, as this is for your eyes only.

SEXUAL CONSENT

This list can change as often as you need. It can change the minute after you give consent to something, if you wish, but I know I'd never considered what I gave consent to until often it was too late. It was a recent sexual partner who always lovingly asked for consent in a super respectful way that made me realise how empowering it was to know your own sexual limitations and have them respected by another.

HOW DO I WANT TO FEEL DURING SEX?

Include things such as pleasure and sexual arousal, but also consider things such as feeling safe, confident and desirable. I'm always really clear about how I want to feel within myself during sex in order to determine whether or not the experience of sex (not necessarily the act of sex itself) is actually satisfying me. Reaching orgasm doesn't always equal feeling safe, respected and desired. Ya feel me?

FURTHER LINES OF ENQUIRY

Ask yourself:

⟨ Am I enjoying sex?

⟨ What's important to me in the bedroom?

⟨ What are my sexual values? We explored values in Chapter 3 if you need a refresher.

Then, you might like to check in with your partner/s and ask them the same questions. I did this and sex got a million times better. You're welcome.

LOVE, SEX & DESIRE AND THE THREE STEPS OF SELF-AWARENESS

I don't know about you, but what I've learned from this chapter is that we often fail to put ourselves first when it comes to love, sex and desire, but it's absolutely paramount that we do. Self-awareness allows us to commit to this by lovingly guiding us to check back in with ourselves often and make sure that our desires are clear to us and are being met.

Step 1: Curiosity

You completed several exercises in this chapter to help you discover what you truly desire in life, love and sex. It was fun, right?! I urge you to get curious with this stuff often, because it will likely shift and change. It's an act of self-love to keep checking in with yourself and ask if your desires are being satisfied. You deserve it. If you're looking for some extracurricular lines of enquiry around love, sex and desire, you might like to look into the following:

★ What have your past relationships taught you about yourself?
★ What stories do you tell yourself about love that perhaps are keeping you stuck?
★ Does the love you have for yourself reflect the way you receive love from another?

Step 2: Acceptance

I'll just speak for myself here, and the teenager who was raised under a Catholic school system. I rejected my own desires for far too long. I viewed them as indulgent, privileged or taboo. For a long time, I didn't think I was worthy of my desires and instead pretended that they weren't mine, therefore I wasn't disappointed if I was unable to manifest them. However, recognising, accepting and owning your desires is an act of self-love. It creates a clear, unadulterated path to manifest a life you truly desire and, as Esther Perel so eloquently put it, '[Desires are] the ultimate expression of our free identity.'

Step 3: Embodiment

It's a curious notion to embody your desires, but if I ask you to visualise someone who embodies their desires, it paints quite the sexy, empowered, liberated and desirable picture, don't you think? Or think of it like this … if you want your desires to move from simply an intention to a full-blown manifestation, then you have to become those desires using the Manifestation Equation as your guide. Allow your thoughts to align with your desires, feel what it's like to already have those desires, take action towards those desires and have faith that you're worthy and deserving of everything you desire in your life. Let this be fuelled through your self-love practice – the way you choose to show up in love and how you express and satisfy yourself between the sheets.

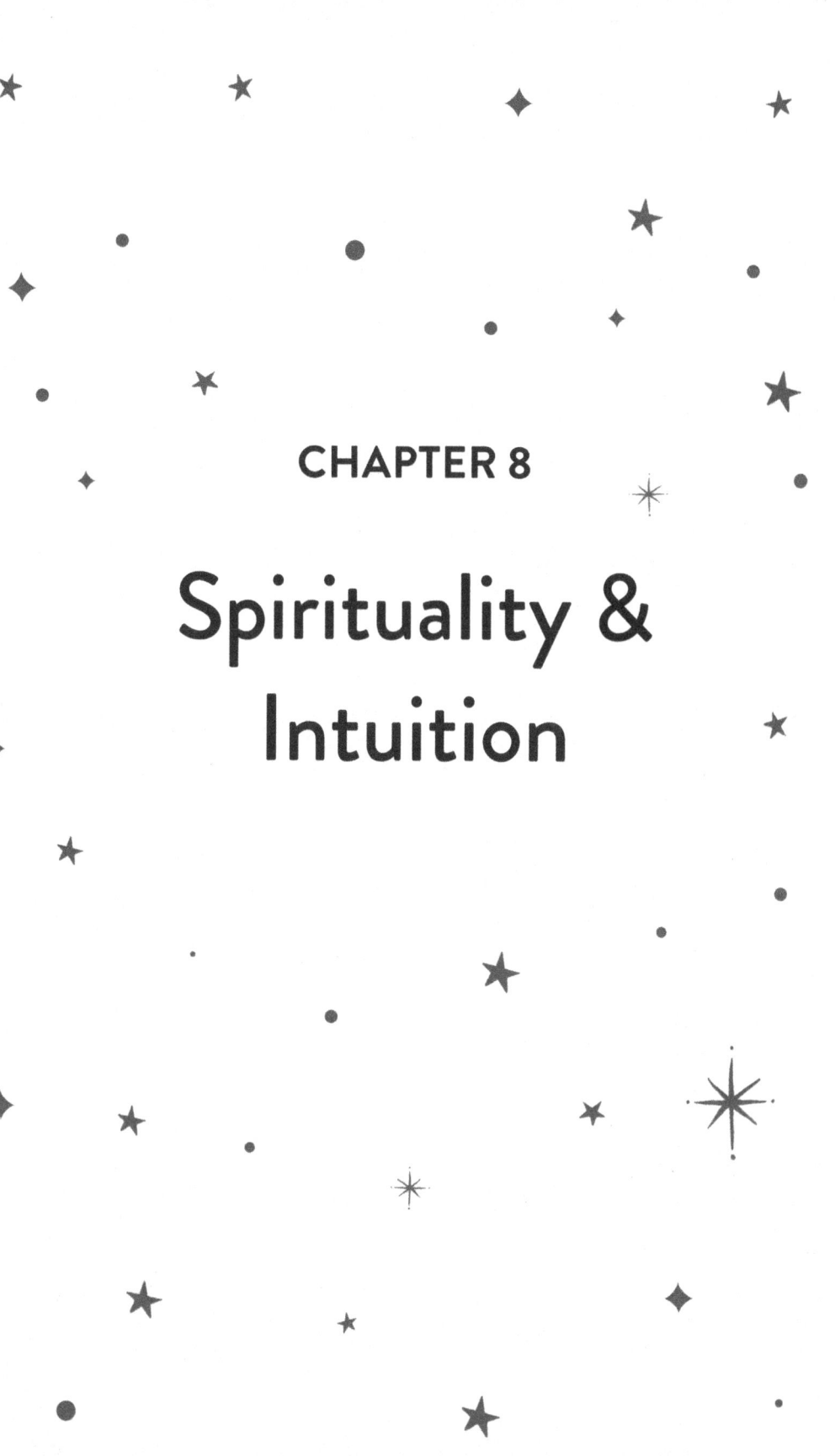

CHAPTER 8

Spirituality & Intuition

Every time a new season of *The Bachelor* launches, there's a cringe-worthy moment. No, it's not the blatantly scripted red carpet introductions disguised as organic meetings, the lack of ethnic and body-size diversity (although these things are cringey AF) or even the blinding white light that emanates from everyone's mouths as they flash their newly whitened grins (and their simultaneous sponsored posts on Instagram). No, it's the woman every season who makes the mistake of mentioning in passing star signs, crystals or dandelion tea and is instantly edited as the airy-fairy hippie with no grip on reality. *Sigh!*

I've rejected this edit my entire life, especially whenever I mention anything that errs on the side of woo woo and could potentially trigger someone into thinking I'm one of 'those' types of new-age spiritual gals. I often do this on dates when men google me to discover my bestselling manifestation book or my podcast about the lunar cycle, or that one time I made the culturally inappropriate mistake of referring to myself as a barefoot gypsy and now that phrase is a seemingly unerasable fixture on the pages of the dark web (read: regular internet).

'I write and teach about spiritual concepts from a really practical point of view,' I begin, 'but I'm NOT woo woo.' This is usually accompanied by some offensive hand gesture and followed with, 'I'm probably the least "spiritual" spiritual person you'll meet.' I often feel a pang of shame after this spiel, because those 'spiritual types' I'm so insistent on distancing myself from aren't bad people or doing spirituality 'wrong', but they're just a tiny aspect of an entire spectrum of what it means to be spiritual. It's unfortunate that in mainstream culture, spirituality is at best depicted with a 'flaky, flighty and frivolous' reputation like the Phoebe Buffays and Dharma Montgomerys of the 90s.

How my relationship with spirituality began might differ from yours. You see, I was born into it. Surrounded by crystals in the birthing suite, I literally exited my mother's vagina to the sounds of the kirtan mantra with an immediate assessment of my natal chart. As a toddler, I was petrified of the dark. I was convinced there were ghosts and monsters hiding in every crevice of my bedroom so to make me feel more secure in my ghost-infested lair, Mum would create a crystal grid around my bed and smudge the room every night before I went to sleep. When I was seven, I was gifted my first deck of angel cards. I used to sit in my room and do readings for my stuffed animals while my mother performed tarot readings in our lounge room for paying customers. I understood the lunar cycle long before I had a menstrual cycle, I prayed each night to the universe (knowing that you had to ask in order to receive), I diagnosed the physical ailments of my friends based on the wisdom of Louise Hay's *You Can Heal Your Life*, and although I didn't quite understand the significance just yet, I knew that there was a bunch of women who ran with the wolves.

When I regale the tales of my upbringing to my adult friends now, they're envious that they weren't raised with the same open-mindedness and bohemian flair. And although I would never take any of it back, I do think my woo-woo childhood is the very reason that I rejected 'the spiritual' for a big chunk in my 30s.

There's a debate among parents that if you introduce alcohol to adolescents before the legal age, then they no longer see it as a prohibited item. This takes the thrill and novelty out of bingeing it and in some cases the teen normalises alcohol so much that they end up avoiding it out of sheer defiance. Spirituality was my booze growing up. It wasn't something I had to discover for myself like many women in their teens and 20s discovering the heart-healing qualities of a rose quartz crystal and hoping it cures all their love woes, or that first oracle deck you buy and use to answer the pressing questions of the day including, 'Should I bother going to work today?' and 'Is he ever going to text me?' Nope, I had boxes of that spiritual guff and I was still just as confused about life as my peers.

In my early 20s, I used spirituality as a prop and as a way to shape my identity – it set me apart from the masses. Who was I without the 'spiritual gal' label I'd inherited growing up? In my late 20s, circa 2012, the spiritual aesthetic became cool. Not in the way that witchcraft got its spot in the limelight with the release of movies such as *The Craft*, *Practical Magic* and *Hocus Pocus* and the rise of shows such as *Charmed* in the 90s, but in the sense that the spiritual aesthetic was no longer just found in dated hippie stores and dark alleyways. It was now commodified in big department stores and regularly featured on cult-blog-turned-wellness-empire Goop. Smudge sticks and spiritual books were gracing the shelves of retail stores such as Urban Outfitters and if you wanted an oracle card pulled, there was an array of Instagram influencers who'd be happy to tell you your fate simply by choosing cards 1, 2 or 3. Spirituality had become a Pinterest board that was being repinned and repurposed into a shadow of its former self.

I remember the exact moment of my spiritual overdose. It was a cold night in June and I'd been dragged into the depths of a rainforest in the pitch black of darkness by a girlfriend who'd insisted that we take part in a full moon ceremony on the eve of my birthday. I'd missed the memo that this ceremony was a) outside in the 12-degree bitter cold, b) on the damp ground so it was best to bring something to sit on and c) would end in an optional (turns out you're not-so-subtly shamed if you don't) naked ecstatic dance. Now, I'm going to stop right here with a caveat and say that I'm in no way ridiculing, making fun of or removing the legitimacy and spirituality from similar ceremonies. I ran new moon ceremonies every month for three years (albeit clothed). THIS one, however, in a rather poetic way, ended up being the catalyst of my rejection of spiritual practices for a few years.

My friend Petal* (she'd appreciate the hippie disguise of her rather conservative birth name) had been part of a Facebook group of 'conscious minded earth goddesses' in the very over-privileged Sydney suburb we lived in. In that group, they'd organise meet-ups, advertise their spiritual events and wares and often talk about spiritual concepts that were perhaps a little taboo to certain people in their friendship groups. It wasn't something I felt like I needed to be a part of but I respected Petal's involve-ment. She'd often beg me to attend their community events but group activities weren't really my thing and my spirituality had always been quite a private and personal practice.

This time was different. I was in the darkest depths of a toxic break-up, I felt like my career was at a complete standstill, I was barely making enough money to afford my rent and my birthday was approaching – an ominous time if you feel your life isn't where it's meant to be. In the previous month out of sheer desperation for answers, I'd been to see a psychic, shamanic healer and reiki master, I'd bought a bunch of new crystals, a smudge stick and a collection of room mists infused with affirmations of love and abundance and I'd read every self-help book I could get my hands on but my life still remained unchanged. This ceremony was the answer! I'd release some stuff into the fire, be blessed by whoever was holding the ceremony and charge my crystals under the light of Mama moon.

About 15 minutes in, the group facilitator – a gorgeous woman in her early 20s – came over and sat down in front of me. She was wearing a crochet triangle bikini top and an ankle-length white muslin flowy skirt (I repeat, 12 degrees, people). On the inside of her left arm was a mandala tattooed onto her pristine tanned skin and pierced through her right nostril was a small emerald stud. Her fingers were adorned with so many crystal rings I was surprised her wrist hadn't snapped from the sheer weight of them, and her long copper hair cascaded over her crochet-covered bosom with perfectly placed kinks that replicated the mane of the goddess Venus in Botticelli's famous painting.

Her piercing blue eyes (which were a tad over-dilated, I might add) looked deep into my soul and she said, 'I'm so glad you're here with us tonight. I felt your energy walk into the space. There's a darkness in you. When was the last time you cleared your chakras?' 'Just last week!' I wanted to spit back at her. Could she not tell I'd seen a shaman AND a reiki master that week? My chakras should be clear AF. But instead, I said nothing and broke down in tears. 'Don't worry, you've come to the right place. We'll heal you.' As she floated back to the group of women, I turned to

Petal. 'I feel like I know her. How do I know her?' Petal looked at me, knowing I was about to make a serious judgement. 'She was on <insert reality TV show of your choosing here>.' I'll keep her reality TV show a secret because I'm not here to throw anyone under the bus.

What woke me up in the most profound of ways that night under the full moon light, my nipples so frozen I swore they could've snapped off, was that I'd never been more disconnected from myself and the only person who had any hope of healing whatever grievances or wounds I possessed was me, definitely not this woman. She'd not embodied her work. It was a regurgitation of spiritual lingo and an adornment of spiritual jewellery but no integration of spirituality in her bones. And I was no better. I realised that in recent years, I'd actually lost my sense of spirituality completely and had replaced it with lots of pretty things that gave the impression of spirituality but had none of its essence. I'd been seeing healer after healer and psychic after psychic, hoping they'd have the answers. I was reading books and understanding the concepts but applying jack shit. I was relying on my crystals to do all the hard work and for the aromatics of my Nag Champa incense to fool everyone, myself included, that I was indeed connected to my spirituality. But really, I was just a lost soul dancing around in her undies in the bitter cold, waiting for someone or something to save her.

In the most extreme way, that full moon circle sent me into a state of rebellion. I went completely cold turkey and abandoned every single practice, tool or association with spirituality. My crystals became purely decor (because, still pretty), my tarot cards were put into a drawer, I stopped setting intentions, I detoxed from seeing any kind of healer or psychic and I didn't pick up another self-help book or spiritual text for two years. In a weird turn of events that no one – not even myself – saw coming, by rejecting all the spiritual tools, I finally discovered the true meaning of spirituality. So perhaps Ms Venus personified did heal me, or at least she woke me the fuck up.

SO, WHAT EXACTLY IS SPIRITUALITY?

If you type that question into Google, you'll get a myriad of dictionary definitions and meanings ranging from 'the quality of being concerned with the human spirit or soul as opposed to material or physical things' to 'sensitivity or attachment to religious values' and 'the state or quality of being dedicated to God, religion, or spiritual things or values, especially as contrasted with material or temporal ones'. I think the attachment of religion to spirituality throws people a little. Some see it as a religious quality, whereas others see it as a rejection of traditional religion. I see it as neither.

Spirituality, for me, at its essence is a deep connection with self and a realisation that there's something more powerful beyond the self. For me, that's the universe. For you, it might be God, Allah, Krishna or Buddha. Perhaps it's just an energy or a knowing. At its heart, it's a realisation that the material and tangible world isn't enough to base our entire belief systems on. You'll see no mention of crystals, smudging wands, incense, purple velvet or floral headpieces. You'll notice that, in fact, two of those definitions speak of the lack of concern for material things. I'm in no way dismissing the relevance or power of these items in the world of spirituality but it's important to be aware that they're tools and adornments of spirituality, not spirituality itself, and in some cases they become a spiritual crutch, as they had for me. If you can tell me your natal chart, the best time to cleanse and charge your crystals and how to clear bad energy from your home but fail to tell me how you feel, what you value and how you act with authenticity and integrity, then you, my friend, are just playing spiritual dress-ups! My main concern with the surplus of spiritual accoutrements is that most of us (read: not all) are using it for external validation, when authentic spirituality is actually about finding the answers within.

My spiritual awakenings have surfaced through life experience. Being met with tragedy, triumph and all the stuff in between. In deep moments of grief, despair and uncertainty that have been contrasted with elation, excitement and unexpected delights. Discovering your own shadows, facing your own fears and sitting in your shit will connect you to your own spirituality more than a stick of palo santo or a shamanic activation mist. Spirituality cannot be given a flat-out definition or meaning because it's unique to the individual's experience.

For me, it's a cauldron of connection and reverence for self, others and the land upon which I reside. It's having an open mind and an open heart. It's being aware that the shadows in life are just as profound as the light when you allow yourself to experience them with grace, kindness and a gentle spirit. In some of my darkest moments, I've found a resilience I didn't know I had, a positivity that I'd convinced myself couldn't exist in such an extreme set of circumstances and the value in internal validation and surrendering in a way I'd never had to before. THIS is spirituality.

Self-awareness is a spiritual practice

If we return to one of the dictionary definitions of spirituality – 'the quality of being concerned with the human spirit or soul as opposed to material or physical things' – it really encapsulates the essence of what self-awareness is. Having a healthy, curious and consistent self-awareness practice deepens your connection with self and in turn connects you deeper to what it means to be spiritual. Hopefully, simply by immersing yourself in the exercises in this book on your quest to make you happen, you've discovered that a spiritual practice is less about the external accessories that are sold to us as spirituality, and rather an understanding and acceptance of who you are. When I wrote *Make It Happen*, I tried to distance manifestation from spirituality. Not because it isn't a spiritual practice (because it is) but I needed readers (i.e. you) to understand that manifestation can't be put into the same basket as crystals, oracle cards and chakra chimes. It's a spiritual practice because it connects you back to self and only once you know who you truly are – at your most authentic – can you fully comprehend what it means to manifest.

Just as we're all unique and independent beings made up of differing thoughts, feelings and energetic capacities, spirituality too is somewhat subjective as it's based on your experience of self. So, let's get curious about your relationship with spirituality.

Unhealthy spirituality looks like:

★ Needing to find meaning in absolutely everything.

★ Creating 'signs' out of nothing. (For example, that number plate has the letters C and J in it and they're the initials of my crush. Even though he has a girlfriend, we're definitely meant to be.)

★ Relying heavily on spiritual tools. (For example, needing to consult your tarot deck before making a decision.)

★ Only feeling 'positive vibes'.

★ Using spiritual excuses such as 'I'm a Scorpio', 'The moon made me do it' or 'It's because Mercury is in retrograde'.

Healthy spirituality looks like:

- ★ Taking responsibility for your own feelings.
- ★ Getting curious about what things mean without attaching to them.
- ★ Using spiritual tools to enhance your connection to self.
- ★ Using spiritual labels to understand yourself better. (For example, because I'm a Gemini I need to be aware of my penchant for gossip.)
- ★ Awareness that spirituality is about embracing a full spectrum of vibrations and feelings.

Spirituality is your willingness to always trust, respect and understand yourself. With a solid sense of self-awareness, you're able to dream big, explore your potential and, most importantly, manifest the life of your dreams. A big component of that is also trusting in something bigger than yourself (i.e. the universe, God or I believe I even offered up Freddie Prinze Jr in *Make It Happen*). The caveat is that you have to be able to trust in both. If you place all of your trust in an external force and none in yourself, then you're missing the entire point (trust me, the universe, God and Freddie all agree with me). So, the next time you find yourself going on a spiritual adventure, reading a spiritual text or subscribing to another spiritual course, ask yourself if it's bringing you closer to understanding yourself or if you're being asked to invest and be validated in something external to you.

INTUITION

I put spirituality and intuition in the same chapter not because I think they're one and the same but because they have one vital thing in common: they both require you to have a deep sense of faith in yourself. As soon as you start reaching for guidance or confirmation externally, you're disconnecting from your self-awareness and your spiritual practices and intuitive knowing will suffer.

How many times have you been told to just 'trust your intuition' when faced with a dilemma or decision? It's easier said than done. It appears to be such a simple solution to all of life's most pressing questions, yet most of us struggle to recognise what it feels like, sounds like and looks like. There's a very logical reason for this: your intuition is unique to you so only you can determine its identifying factors.

Intuition, at its most basic level, is your ability to understand something instinctively, without conscious or analytical reasoning. You know when you just *know*? That's your intuition. Some people are convinced theirs isn't as fine-tuned as others but, the truth is, we all have the same capacity to access our intuition. The problem is that most of us are drowning our intuition by reaching externally for the answers. To truly understand your own inner guidance system, you need to understand the pitfalls of external validation.

External validation (EV) versus internal validation (IV)

I always see this as a WWE throwdown. Your intuition is doing its best to stay alive, relevant and dominant, but it's no match for external validation. If EV is in the ring, then EV will win. The only way for your intuition to walk away a champion is for it to be in the ring on its own. If that analogy confused you, don't sweat it. Instead, know this: if trusting your intuition is important to you and you want it to be strong and trustworthy AF, then you must quit seeking validation outside of yourself.

What is external validation?

When you have a dilemma that you're trying to solve, are you the kind of person who'll run it past a million different people? Or perhaps you're so terrified of making the wrong decision that you prefer to ask others so that the onus is on them. Or maybe it's just that you have zero faith in yourself to make the correct decision and have much more faith in the people around you. If you answered yes to any of those statements, let me say, 'Hey, welcome to the normal people club,' but also, 'You gotta stop!'

Searching for validation outside of yourself – be it from people, experiences or successes – is a recipe for disaster when it comes to trusting your intuition. Trying to recognise and follow your intuition can be tricky enough as it is but when you purposefully turn to the external to confirm, decide or make choices on your behalf, not only are you completely bypassing your intuition but you're also choosing to ignore, deny and disagree with it. Which, if you were your own intuition, you'd think was pretty rude. Amirite?

So, let's start by getting curious about your relationship with external validation.

Exercise 34

EXTERNAL VALIDATION

Grab your self-awareness journal and answer these questions as honestly as possible. Remember, it's normal to look for the answers outside of yourself, but just because it's normal, it doesn't mean it's the best option. Only once you recognise your relationship with external validation can you truly understand why trusting yourself is always the better option.

Answer the following questions:

1. Do I struggle with external validation?

2. Where do I seek external validation? For example, I used to constantly seek it at work.

3. Why do I seek validation externally? Be honest with yourself.

4. Who do I seek external validation from? Friends? Family? Strangers on the internet?

A lifetime of psychics and all I got was this crappy T-shirt

I used to have an addiction to seeing psychics. Whether you believe in psychics or not doesn't matter to this story but the reason I saw psychics was because I believed they possessed a talent for reading energy and 'knowing' how things were going to turn out, which was a skill I didn't think I had. It was a version of outsourcing but it was also a way for me to settle my nerves regarding how my future would play out. One of my best friends is a psychic and my mum used to work as a psychic. I have an annual check-in session with a particular psychic each year and another psychic who I text for a spur-of-the-moment appointment when I'm in a particular spiritual dilemma. So no one come at me while I tell you about my beef with psychics, okay?

Every single psychic I've ever seen has told me the exact same things about my life, which makes me confident of their accuracy. Some of the things have happened. Some of them haven't happened (yet). On the day of my reading and in the days that follow, I feel confident and trusting of what they've said to me, which is why we see psychics, right? They put our fears at ease, give us hope and something to look forward to and, even if just briefly, you feel as if everything is going to be fine. Then, roughly a week later when none of that stuff has happened (which, FYI, is normal, plus accurate timelines are near impossible to predict), we start to doubt what we were told and we consider making an appointment with a different psychic. Essentially, we start to search for external validation that everything is going to be A-okay from another source as extra weight and proof that what they said was true.

Seeing psychics serially is a representation of our own inability to trust ourselves and have faith that we're the creators of our own future. If you truly believe that manifestation is possible for you – if you have faith that if it's not this, it'll be something better – then turning to a psychic for confirmation every couple of months is just a big red flag that says, 'I don't trust myself'. Think about when you make an appointment with a psychic. It's not when you feel happy, calm and confident. It's when you feel anxious, worried and devoid of hope. (Well, it is for me anyway.)

So, this year I've pulled back and asked myself, 'Why are you booking this reading? Is it because you need someone else to validate your future? Do you not have faith that you're the one that manifests the life you desire?' Hmm, well I've written a couple of books about it … My point? I respect psychics and the work they do and I value their service when we approach it from the right place but when we don't, it's just another form of external validation that's no different from constantly asking your friends for their opinions so you don't have to make decisions on your own.

It's a natural human tendency to want approval and confirmation from your peers (and paid professionals). But at the heart of seeking the approval of others is the belief that your self-worth lies in the hands of others, rather than your own, and that they know what's best for you over your own judgement.

External validation comes down to three things:

1. **Low self-worth.** Harsh, but true. If you valued yourself, then why would you need the approval of others?

2. **Inability to trust your own instincts.** If you're questioning yourself constantly, then it's time to build a more trustworthy relationship with yourself – just as you'd want to build a trusting relationship with a partner.

3. **A lack of self-awareness.** Nobody knows yourself better than you do, and if they do, then you've got some more self-awareness work to do.

I'm going to go out on a limb and say that you're pretty much all over point three, correct? So then you must ask yourself if you're seeking answers externally because you don't trust yourself or because you don't feel worthy enough. It might be both but either way, know this: when we seek answers externally, it's because on some level we doubt our own judgement, opinions and emotions. Self-doubt is the antithesis of trusting your own instincts. By learning to listen to your intuition and then act on it, you're prioritising your most accurate guidance system: YOU!

Think about the reasons why you trust a friend, lover or close work colleague. It's likely because you know them really well, you don't doubt them, you respect them and you probably even love them (at the very least, like them very much). These are the things you must be able to cultivate within yourself in order to strengthen your intuition. The good news is that everything you have learned up to this point has been leading you towards a greater sense of self-awareness and a deeper trust in who you are and what you're capable of. When you can understand how you identify, emote, exert energy, communicate, love and desire, you can better trust that you're capable of making the best choices for you! If you can love and accept yourself (despite ...), then seeking validation will be ten times more rewarding.

Ways to internally validate yourself:

★ Commit to becoming self-aware. Consider that box ticked.
★ Check in with your values. You wrote these back in Chapter 4.

★ Be kind to yourself. You don't always have to know the answer or even have the right answer but be kind and gentle with yourself while you try and figure it out.

★ Feel it in your body. If something isn't sitting right with you, you'll be able to feel it in your body. It might be a sensation in your gut, a sinking feeling in your chest or sweaty palms. The better you get to know yourself, the more familiar these sensations will become.

★ Be accountable for your own actions. Eeep! This is likely the reason that most of you seek validation externally – you don't have to take responsibility if things don't work out. Well unless, dear reader, you're under the age of 18, you're an adult and it's time to take some self-responsibility.

★ Always ask yourself first. I'm not saying that you can't turn to people for advice or their opinion, as this is a massive part of forming meaningful connections with people. However, before you ask anyone else, decide what outcome or answer you think is the wisest one first.

Accessing your intuition

Unfortunately, there's no checklist, formula or guidebook I can provide you for working with your intuition. Perhaps this is why we reach externally, as it's a little more black and white than trying to interpret how we really feel about something. It puts the responsibility on someone or something else. Like I said before, your intuition is unique to you. This means that the way it speaks to you, indicates what it's feeling and alerts you to the path best for you will be different for everyone. I'm not sure if we ever actually strengthen our intuition; I think we just get better at listening to it, not ignoring it and learning to trust it above anything else.

Familiarising yourself with your intuition takes time. For some people it's a deep inner knowing, for others it's a physical feeling and some folk say they hear a very clear message, while others just have a gut instinct that they can't ignore. I have a few different techniques for listening to my intuition that might be of assistance to you, but first, let's get curious about how you access your intuition.

Exercise 35
ACCESSING YOUR INTUITION

How do you communicate with your intuition? Grab your self-awareness journal and note down some of the ways your intuition speaks to you. Here are some questions to prompt you:

1. Do I ask my intuition for the answers?

2. How does my intuition respond?

3. Do I see signs?

4. Is my intuition a feeling in my heart, gut or somewhere else?

5. Do I hear a response from my intuition or see a visualisation in my mind?

6. Do I just know things without a doubt?

Intuition hacks!

My intention was to let you know that the next few tricks to help understand your intuition better will feel like you've just discovered a secret recipe your nonna has been hiding from the family for centuries, or in the context of that unfortunate headline, like you've just uncovered a new biohacking technique on an episode of Joe Rogan's podcast that you simply can't live without.

Not all of these 'hacks' will resonate with you, and that's okay. For now, you're just getting curious about how your intuition speaks to *you*.

Ask your higher self a question

Ever heard of automatic writing? It's a way of writing without conscious intention. It's best to not overthink it and instead just give it a go:

1. Grab a pen and paper and set yourself up in a safe and comfortable space.

2. Write down on the piece of paper a question you
   need the answer to.
3. Close your eyes and centre yourself in any way
   that feels good for you. It could be a few deep breaths
   or a deep meditation – whatever feels good in your
   body.
4. Ask your higher self the question on the piece of paper.
5. Open your eyes and start writing a response on the
   piece of paper. The trick is to not think, just write.
   Trust that what's coming through is your intuitive
   knowing. Often, I'm so dumbfounded about what
   comes through.

The inside/outside rule

When working with intuition, often people get stumped inter-
preting whether it's their intuition telling them what to do or if
it's their ego, anxiety or an outside influence. I can totally relate,
which is why I came up with this brilliant rule. Understanding
the inside/outside rule is all about tuning into your own energy.

When your intuition is whispering to you, it feels as if the
energy is coming from inside of you and radiating out. The
feeling is expansive, nourishing and often exhilarating, as if a
weight has been lifted. When it's your ego, anxiety or an outside
influence, it feels as if the energy is coming towards you from
the outside. The feeling is heavy, restrictive, depleting and often
just feels off. The descriptive words might be different for you
but the next time you're not sure who has the microphone, tune
into the energy and decide if it's coming from the inside out or
the outside in.

Feel it in your body

This one resonates with most people I share it with. Let's say you need to make a decision between option A and option B. You're going to sit with both options for a period of time as if you committed to one and see how it feels in your body. You could sit with it for a couple of minutes, an hour or an entire day – it's up to you. If I have the time, I like to sleep on it. I think the morning after you've made a decision is always really telling. How do you feel when you first wake up?

Let's start with option A. You tell yourself this is the decision that's been made. Check in with how you feel. What emotions arise? What is your mind doing? How's your breathing? Is the energy coming from inside or outside? Sit with this decision for as long as you need. Now, you do the same with option B. They'll feel different in your body.

MANIFESTATION REMINDER

Your intuition is never wrong. It'll always lead you to where you're meant to be, even if it doesn't feel like it at first. Trust yourself. You know what's what.

Practice makes pretty good

I've ignored my intuition too many times to count. Just this year, I ignored it in several damaging ways. However, every time I suffer the consequences of ignoring what I know to be true, I get better at listening and embracing its wisdom next time. That is what a good intuition practice is: making mistakes and then doing better. Knowing the right thing to do and then purposefully choosing the other option out of fear, short-term gain or because everyone else thinks they know what's best is a bitch in the moment but also confirmation that deep down you really did know what was best. I always get a major kick out of that. I want you to as well! You might like to consider starting an intuition journal where you document your intuitive feelings and whether or not you followed what you thought to be true, and what the consequences were of that. It can be a really clear way of recognising that you really do know yourself better than anyone else.

SPIRITUALITY & INTUITION AND THE THREE STEPS OF SELF-AWARENESS

I left this chapter until last because spirituality and intuition are the epitome of self-awareness. One cannot have a spiritual practice without first having an awareness of who they are, just as one can't trust their intuition if they don't trust and know themselves inside and out. It's a bloody relief, don't you think? All that's required to be spiritual and in tune with your intuition is to be aware of yourself. Piece of cake.

Step 1: Curiosity

I trust that a lot came to light for you in this chapter around what spirituality isn't, and if you're anything like me that likely brought you some peace. The same goes for your intuition. Isn't it a relief to find out there's not some big trick to being more intuitive and that it's just about liking, trusting and respecting yourself more? If you're looking for some extracurricular lines of enquiry around your spiritual and intuitive self, you might like to look into the following:

★ After each of your current spiritual practices, ask yourself how you feel and whether or not the reward of connecting deeper with self is being met or not.
★ Could you go an entire week without validating yourself externally? I tried this experiment and it was wild how difficult it was. It made me realise how unnecessarily we turn to the external for answers and acceptance.

Step 2: Acceptance

Acceptance is a spiritual practice. Every time you learned about a new aspect of self-awareness in this book and embraced the essence of who you are, you were strengthening your spirituality. Every time you accept that you have both strengths and weaknesses and choose to love and trust yourself because of them, you connect deeper with your intuition. Self-awareness teaches us that we can't grow and expand if we can't first accept who we are right now.

Step 3: Embodiment

If you can commit to embodying and practising your self-awareness not just while reading this book but for the rest of your existence, then you'll always be aligned with what you spiritually value, trust, want and believe in. Part of this is not just listening to your intuition but also trusting it and following it, knowing that it might not always lead you to where you desire to go but it will always lead you to a place you need to be.

CHAPTER 9

Now What?

So, you know how I began this book with a rant about self-help and personal-development books? And you got all confused because you were like, 'Umm I believe this is one?' And I was like, 'It might look like one, but it's different.' Remember that? Well, here's why …

This isn't a self-help or personal-development book. It's an advanced manifestation manual that has taken you deep inside yourself so that you can get curious, accept and embody who you are at your essence. No development or help necessary. The best bit? You've been doing the 'work' along the way (you have, right?). The exercises throughout this book have opened you up to parts of yourself that have always been there but perhaps you ignored them, convinced yourself you weren't worthy of them or just didn't know where to look. The good news is that now that you're conscious of the process of self-awareness, it'll come naturally to you as you continue throughout your life. And the best news? Your manifestation practice is going to completely transform.

It works like this:

1. Only by knowing who you truly are can you get clarity around what you truly want to manifest for yourself.
2. The person that you show up as in all of the six aspects of self contributes to your personal vibration.
3. That vibration is responsible for the things that you attract into your life.

4. From this place, you're able to set intentions with clarity and they'll be aligned with who you are at your most authentic.

Because here's the thing ... if you're setting intentions for things you want to manifest but you're not in alignment with yourself, then it's going to be near impossible for them to come to fruition. However, when you can become so self-aware that you're just showing up every day as an authentic version of you – aligning your thoughts, feelings, actions and faith with what you desire – well, it's likely you won't even need to set intentions because you'll be the living, breathing, take-responsibility-for-my-actions embodiment of your own potential. It's pretty crazy, sexy, cool, huh?

It will, however, involve:

★ Regular self-reflection. This could be done in a journal, talking it out with a trusted confidant or just being conscious of it in your thought patterns and feelings. Unless you're regularly checking in with yourself and evaluating your role in your own life, then the work you've done around self-awareness will slowly slip away. Remember, this is a lifelong practice, but it will become more natural and easeful #promise.

★ Staying aligned with your values. It's one thing writing down your values in your self-awareness journal but it takes a self-aware person to stay aligned with them. Also, it's important to remember that your values can change over time so a regular check-in to see if they're still relevant is crucial.

★ Leaning into your strengths and making room for your weaknesses. We looked at your strengths and weaknesses across many different aspects of self and concluded that an awareness of a weakness instantly makes it a strength, as long as you're using it as a signal that perhaps there's a different way to do things.

★ Accepting your uniqueness and recognising uniqueness in others. One of the most beneficial things about self-awareness is that it makes us more aware of our own individuality and the individuality of those around us. As you accept and love yourself more, a flow-on effect is that you have more love and acceptance for others.

★ Knowing that actions speak louder than words. I made a big song and dance about the action part of the Manifestation Equation in *Make It Happen,* and I think it deserves an equally performative cabaret act when it comes to self-awareness. It's one thing to know things about yourself – even to accept them – but if you're not taking actions towards the things you want to manifest in your life based on your own awareness then, dearest friend of mine, you're just all bloody talk. This is why embodiment – the final step in the three steps of self-awareness – is so crucial, and it's something that will shift and change as you do, so you have to keep checking in.

Self-awareness is ultimately a deeper connection with you because who you are is injected into everything that you do. Why wouldn't you want to nurture it, cultivate it and embody the bejesus out of it? Anaïs Nin once wrote, 'We don't see things as they are, we see them as we are.' I believe this means that you can't have clarity around how you perceive and interact with the world unless you're clear on who you are because who you are puts a unique filter on all of your perceptions.

The six aspects of self provide a beautiful framework for your own self-discovery. They're the key areas in which we can reflect on ourselves as a whole being, but self-awareness stems so much further. It's a checking in with self when making decisions and navigating relationships, as well as when facing failures and successes. It's a recognition that you have the opportunity to take responsibility for how your life unfolds, and all of the tools are already at your disposal. That's such a relief, isn't it? All that you require is the ability to go inward and get curious.

If you've read either of my previous books, you'll know that part of the writing process for me is that I live everything I'm writing as I'm writing it. It was refreshing with this book because, as I mentioned at the commencement of this tale, I had quite a bit of work to do to come back to self after losing a big part of my identity earlier in the year. I swung from numbing out my emotions to experiencing them all at once. I found it difficult to articulate my words and communicate on a basic level. I had zero energy for myself and others. I had no desire for the future, certainly no desire to love or be loved, and I'd rejected any love for self as punishment for the person I'd become. To top it all off, I'd lost my sense of connection – with self and others but mostly with the universe, which is something that had always been of great comfort to me.

However, as I wrote each chapter of this book, my connection with self slowly started to re-form. I (re)discovered the parts of myself that felt incredibly true to me. I reconnected with my values and chose to identify with the innate parts of my personality and the things that light me up. I rediscovered that I have a natural tendency to apply logic to my emotions but they're far more efficiently processed when I allow myself to fully feel them – this shifted my vibration big time.

By the time I got to the energy chapter, I realised that what I needed more than anything was lots and lots of proper rest. Once I allowed my system to fully let go and surrender to doing nothing, my energy returned. I'd become lazy with my communication and, as I wrote about all the different styles and types of communication, I realised that I hadn't been playing to my strengths and had instead slipped into being a passive bystander. So, I reconnected with my verbal communication skills, became conscious of my non-verbal cues and practised being more assertive in my delivery.

By the time I got to the love, sex and desire chapter, I felt like my personal vibration had picked up some serious juice. I'm not sure if it was a manifestation or pure luck (it was definitely a manifestation) but I found myself in a rather delightful exploration of my sexuality with a very respectful, consensual and, dare I say, desirable lover. He reminded me not only of my own desires for self, love and sex but that there's so much power in recognising them, acknowledging them and then sharing them with another.

As I approached the chapter on spirituality and intuition, I was feeling apprehensive. I knew that through my recent experience, I'd battled with both the idea of spirituality and trusting in my own wisdom. I'd been let down by both but as I moved through that chapter, it dawned on me, like I hope it did for you, that you can only be let down by that which is external to you. When you flip the narrative on spirituality to be about a deeper connection with self, it's evident that the first five aspects brought more spirituality into my life than any moon circle, crystal grid or smoking smudge stick ever could.

As for intuition, well, once I was able to reconnect with myself, have full awareness of who I was and learn to love myself again, internally validating and trusting myself felt easeful and natural. Then, when the book was finished, something incredible happened. With very little effort on my part, two intentions that I'd been working on for two years manifested seemingly overnight. I kid you not! This is the power of self-awareness.

If you've arrived here at the final chapter while doing the exercises along the way, the magic is already unfolding. Simply by exploring, getting curious, accepting and embodying who you are as you flipped through each page of this book, you became more self-aware than when you began. You're a different person to the one who began this adventure. A natural by-product of this is that you'll find things will naturally start to manifest for you as your vibration comes into alignment with who you truly are. It really is the most effortless way to manifest, and all it took was a commitment to make YOU happen.

Acknowledgements

This book started as a bunch of individual essays and then slowly morphed itself into a follow-up title to *Make It Happen*. It was never my intention, but it turned out to be a natural progression.

In order to get this book to where it is today, I hid myself away from the world – not as a recluse, but as a writer who wanted to dive back into her own teachings to give her words the authenticity they required. While many of us had no choice but to isolate, with government-imposed lockdowns and border closures limiting our movements in 2021, I chose to isolate even when freedoms were restored in order to get to know myself (again) and also to get these words into some sort of sensical order. So, unlike the acknowledgements in my previous books, I'll keep this one brief, because the truth is I didn't cross paths with many people during the writing process other than my barista and the Woolies delivery guy.

I'm about to officially enter a terrain I've approached with trepidation until now out of fear of being slapped with labels such as 'crazy cat lady', but I couldn't possibly have written this book without my loyal writing companion Poppy. She is a rescue kitten with a heart of gold who changed my life in unexpected ways and plays the role of grief companion, snuggle buddy, fun facilitator and smile inducer. Her two favourite resting places in the mornings while I write are directly in front of the computer screen and on top of my keyboard – not at all helpful, but adorable nonetheless. As someone who always publicly declared herself team dog in the cat vs dog debate, I can officially say that Poppy has won me over to the feline side.

Domestic animals aside, the most integral and important thank you goes to my publisher Kelly Doust. This is our third book together in the space of four years – can you believe it? Kelly, your belief in me and my book ideas is something for which I am forever grateful. Bringing me with you to Affirm Press was such an incredible honour and privilege, and I'm so grateful to always have you in my corner (especially when I call you in 'I can't do this' and 'it's not working' moments).

A big thank you to my new home at Affirm Press. Martin and Keiran, it's an honour to be included among your talented portfolio of authors, and your warm welcome as I made the transition to a new publishing house has been much appreciated. To the rest of the Affirm Press team, thank you for welcoming me with open arms. I'm excited to work with you all.

A big shout out to Alissa Dinallo for another incredible, Insta-worthy book cover. As much as we resist the cliché, we all judge a book by its cover, and I'm forever grateful that you continue to create covers that draw people in even before they've read the blurb.

Lastly, I'd like to acknowledge the readers and celebrators of my first book, *Make It Happen*. Without you, this book wouldn't exist. Your emails, DMs, voice notes and comments never go unnoticed. Hearing about all of the wonderful things that you've manifested using the Manifestation Equation brings me an incredible amount of joy, so please never stop sharing your experiences with me. Hopefully, there are many more to come after devouring *Make You Happen*.